FROM MY CENTURY TO YOURS: WISDOM FROM THE NEAR 100-YEAR LIFE OF FORMER CONGRESSMAN NEAL EDWARD SMITH

"I enjoyed reading Congressman Smith's memoir. It brought back a lot of my own memories. Neal Smith has always treated the Des Moines Register's reporters and editors with great respect and has been very helpful to us over the years, and our respect towards him has been mutual. I still remember the first time I called Congressman Smith's office and asked for his press secretary, and I was told he didn't have a press secretary, which is a situation I hadn't encountered before or since. Congressman Smith was chairing a House committee meeting that day, and they recessed briefly so he could come to the phone and answer my questions for a news story. That was classic Neal Smith – unpretentious and sincere.

I have a lot of memories of Congressman Smith regularly visiting the Des Moines Register's offices at 7th and Locust Street in downtown Des Moines. You could usually find him sitting in a chair next to political columnist Jim Flansburg's desk, or talking with chief political reporter David Yepsen or our editorial writers to make sure they understood why an policy issue was important to Iowans. If I needed a question answered, I could stop him and get some answers.

Those were times when politics were not so polarized and when both Republicans and Democrats were more willing to find common ground to do what was best for Iowa. Even in recent years, long after he left Washington, D.C., I have interviewed Congressman Smith on occasion for stories and when I have done so I have often heard from from readers afterwards who have found his perspectives worthwhile and timeless."

Sincerely,

BILL PETROSKI
FORMER STAFF WRITER DES MOINES REGISTER

From My Century to Yours

WISDOM FROM THE NEAR 100-YEAR LIFE OF FORMER CONGRESSMAN NEAL EDWARD SMITH

bpc

From My Century to Yours: Wisdom From the Near 100-Year Life of Former Congressman Neal Edward Smith is published by Business Publications Corporation Inc., an Iowa corporation.

Copyright © 2019 by Neal Smith.

ISBN-13: 978-0-9986528-8-7
Library of Congress Control Number: 2019933534
Business Publications Corporation Inc., Des Moines, IA

Business Publications Corporation Inc.
The Depot at Fourth
100 4th Street
Des Moines, Iowa 50309
(515) 288-3336

CONTENTS

PREFACE

I have lived all but one year of a century. My century started on March 23, 1920, and upon reflection, I believe it has seen more important changes and developments both good and bad than occurred in any other ten centuries of human existence.

There are thousands of changes and developments we now consider "good" that have made life more enjoyable for the species, but some of what we so far have considered good have increased effects on the lives of the human species of the future.

Two of those changes we could consider "progress" that I would argue have devastating effects on the future of the world both have to do with humankind's tendency for destruction: (1) the ability of few people to kill masses of people; and (2) the huge increase in the problems we face due to the way the human species has thrown nature out of balance.

The days in which rifle companies faced one another and outcomes of a war were mostly determined by which side had the most soldiers, or even the most small weapons, are past. Nuclear explosives and the ability of an individual to shoot down helicopters while hiding in tall grass ended old methods of war.

Nature can no longer bring itself back into balance because the destruction of entire species is too great. We destroy much faster than nature can re-create. When I was born in 1920, the world population was estimated at two billion. Today it is estimated at 6.5 billion or more and ever-increasing, and the increase in population is not on level with resource production. The ever-increasing population consumes far more than the earth can produce.

As world leaders and historians have always told us, in determining what we should expect and do in the future, we must be aware of the events and occurrences of the past that collectively determined how we got where we are today. In this story of my life, I will explain some of the history I remember that collectively determined just how we got here. Except for specific dates, which I secured from the World Almanac, this dissertation comes entirely from my own memory.

one

Back to the Beginning

Neal Edward Smith
Born March 23, 1920
Hedrick, Iowa

I lived my first twenty years with parents who were working amid an economy that went from boom to bust. I was born in 1920, two years after World War I ended and just before a big boom in which the price of corn reached $5 a bushel and prosperity was assumed to be permanent. What followed, however, was a terrible depression when corn plummeted to $.25 per bushel and many citizens of the U.S. questioned seriously whether the free enterprise system was the best option.

I am told that with the economic boom, and the "untouchable" feeling that turned out to be false, there came a big change in social conduct—such as women showing their flesh, increased prostitution, bootlegging when alcohol was outlawed, a big division between city and farm community people, and an increase in crime.

Instead of being a part of the social changes that occurred in the early 1920s, my parents were just returned from a homesteading stint in Montana. They had suffered serious health problems and ended up deep in debt for health costs. My father had a boil. The accepted medical procedure was to keep it covered with Denver mud so it would not come to a head and drain. That caused the infection to enter his blood system and he had to have a kidney removed. He was in a hospital for ninety days. Nowadays we use plants and herbs for medicinal purposes like this, but doctors of the day ridiculed Native Americans for using such things. They thought they were well informed, and their lack of knowledge left my father without a kidney and my family deep in debt. This experience made me extremely interested in and willing to offer strong support for medical research when I was in Congress many years later.

When immigrants from Europe had chased the natives off the land in the 1800s and settled in Iowa, they settled by communities. Those from one country and with the same ideas and prejudices would settle in one community and form one town, while those from another country with another set of prejudices would settle in another area. Prejudices dictated community. I held some of those prejudices until I enlisted in the army with boys who were from New York and other cities and towns all over the United States. They had numerous religious affiliations and were of various races and creeds. It was an eye-opening experience, and it changed me almost completely. Due to that experience, I very strongly supported Civil Rights and equal opportunity legislation in Congress.

The response of the "winners" of WWI was to punish the losers (Germany) and make them pay for the aftermath of the war. In other words, we "winners" decided it necessary to dwell on the past. Individual countries in Europe were left with borders they needed to protect from their neighbors, which was just the opposite of what occurred after WWII with the establishment of NATO, which included Germany and looked toward the best future.

WWI had cost our government $32 billion, and it had been able to sell bonds to pay for half of it only because an amendment to the Constitution permitting taxation according to the level of income that had been passed in 1913. This also became very important during the recession of the 1930s and since. The Hawley-Smoot Tariff Law was passed in 1930 and caused the stock market to bust worse than any recession ever before. It was rescinded, but the experience has been cited often as a reason to support trade bills and oppose tariffs.

———

The following is an excerpt from my first book, <u>Mr. Smith Went to Washington</u>, published in 1996.

I was born on March 23, 1920 in the house my great-grandfather built in Keokuk County, Iowa. He had migrated from Indiana shortly after the Blackhawk war was settled, opening up a second new large territory in Iowa for homesteaders. When I was born, may parents were living temporarily with my father's parents. My parents had come back to Iowa from the Montana homestead because there was no school in the area for my brother and sister to attend. By then my brother and sister were six and seven years old and ready to start.

My grandfather had homesteaded in Ness County, Kansas and had moved back to Iowa for similar reasons. Although my grandfather did not have a highschool education, he was a good mathematician. He could estimate weights of animals fast and with great accuracy, and he was a successful horse and mule trader and cattle buyer. He also kept stallions and jacks for service for a fee. He believed strongly in education. His seven children were from one of only two families in that whole community who attended college. Several of my father's seven siblings attended college one year and then had to teach in a country school one year (a highschool education was all that was required) to earn enough money to attend another year, but they were encouraged to do so. My father attended Drake University and had completed all but one year toward a medical degree before the Drake University School of Medicine closed. However, he was qualified to be a pharmacist, which he became before homesteading in Montana.

My family had a history of being encouraged to look ahead, to pioneer or homestead, that is, to have visions of a better future. As it turned out, I needed that encouragement.

There was a smokehouse on a neighboring forty acres that my father farmed. The house had burned down, but the smokehouse, which was more like a wash shed of about ten feet by eighteen feet was still there along, with a well. When I was about thirteen years old, an unemployed bachelor who had been a millwright at Quaker Oats in Cedar Rapids, Iowa, moved into the building. He lined it with paper and made a stove out of an old barrel. My parents would give him cracked eggs, and he had some very small potatoes that were picked from potato fields after the sellable ones had been gathered. He boiled enough little potatoes for a week and mixed a few with an egg a couple times a day. Thus, his diet was largely potatoes and eggs, but my parents would also give him some canned goods.

I liked to go visit with him. I will never forget going with him to the mailbox one day. He took the mail out of the box, opened an envelope and started dancing a jig. He was so happy. He had just received his first $15 old-age pension check. Afterward, he told my parents he had had less than $2 left and had assumed he would soon have to go on the road as a hobo. I have never forgotten that experience. After a few years, President Franklin Roosevelt finally succeeded in passing the Social Security Act, and later the Iowa Legislature started using the revenue *from the 2 percent sales tax for other purposes, even though it had been passed with the promise of using a good share of it to assist the elderly.*

In 1931, Hoover approved a $700,000 increase budget for public works and supported the famous Hoover Dam, but he was opposed to spending for poverty relief until just before the election season in 1932. Labor leaders actually said a revolution was possible if food was not made available. Food trucks were being stopped and robbed in some states. WWI vets had been promised a bonus to be delivered in 1945 when most of them were in their late 50s or 60s. When hard times hit, many pushed to receive the bonus earlier. The drive ended in a large march and gathering in Washington, D.C. Douglas MacArthur was a top general in the army at the time, and he drove them out. I remember hearing about General MacArthur but I certainly never dreamed I would someday serve in a war in which he was in top control in the Pacific.

In 1932, Democrat Clyde Herring was elected Governor of Iowa. He was the first democrat to be elected in Iowa since the Civil War, except for one in the 1800s. Under Herring's leadership, the legislature passed a law sending $15 per month to poor residents around the state. That money was critical for those who could not travel to soup lines. It was financed with a two percent sales tax. Counties in Iowa set up a "county farm" as a place of last resort for the poor. The one in Polk County was still operating after WWII and was like most of the others with two barracks, one for men and one for women. The cots were side by side in big rooms and had indoor toilets. They raised and preserved food in the summer to consume in the winter. They raised milk cows, chickens, and hogs, and the residents worked the farms.

Farm programs were developed in the depth of the depression. Millions of people were hungry. Many people lived as bums,

At the farm 2 miles east of Packwood. From left to right, my sister, me with a tricycle, Pampel, Alvin Sheet, Fred Sewers, Jim Smith (father).

having left home to knock on doors and beg, including those in the country because they knew farmers raised gardens and canned and preserved food for winter consumption. There was simultaneously not enough demand for the crops farmers sold and a shortage of food for the unemployed. During the depression, people became convinced that farm programs were not just meant to help in an emergency situation but that food and fiber production required national programs at all times.

Between 1923 and 1929, 23 percent of middle-income jobs had been replaced by technology. There was a 25 percent unemployment rate. This was repeated from 1988 to 2000 when 30 percent of factory assembly line workers were replaced by technology. Workers were then unable to find employment and the cost of living increased as the income shifted to those who owned the technology. The workers replaced by technology need retraining in order to do a job that had not yet been replaced by technology. Tractors replaced horses and mules in the 1930s, which decreased the number of farmers needed to produce a crop and replaced demand for feed for the livestock with a market for tractor fuel.

Electric gadgets, like radios, were becoming popular in the late 1930s, but there was no electricity on farms in Iowa. The Rural Electric Administration was born in that decade. A private electric line went past the farm where we lived, but the Electric Company did not want to be bothered with small time rural households. The electric company wanted $1,000 per customer to secure service; that was the price of a small farm. The line went from Packwood to Ollie and we lived on the road between the two towns. They did not want to serve rural customers, and they successfully opposed an REA line on our road. The first time I ever had electricity or plumbing in the house I lived in was when I went into the army in March of 1942.

Until 1935, when my family acquired its first radio, the only entertainment my parents had on the farm was to read books or weekly newspapers or to go to town on Saturday nights and loaf in front of the grocery stores with other members of the community. Children would walk the streets and listen to the old folks' conversations. Until I was about twelve years old, I didn't fully understand what they were saying. I remember when I was eight, the adults were all in agreement that they had to vote for Hoover because Al Smith was a Catholic. But then, four years later, they were all against Hoover. They had vehement prejudices against other people and hated other people just because they were different. Of course, they were always willing to change their tune...if it was in their best interests. My sister was an expert violin player. We went to the Christian church and she was invited to play her violin at a Methodist church gathering. People in our church were mad because she played at the other church. People were always looking for something they could complain about that would make them feel and appear superior to everyone else.

I was old enough at the time when I was living in a home with very poor parents to remember the lift that occurred when Franklin Delano Roosevelt became president and delivered speeches over the radio. He called them Fireside Chats. I was thirteen years old, and I remember many of those speeches and the way they encouraged people. We would hear the announcement about when the speech was going to occur and we would go to the stores where store owners would turn up the radio so they could hear FDR speak. That was when adults, and even children like me, started believing government could be helpful to the people of the country and could make our future brighter; it no longer seemed just an expense we had to abide with to pay for the army and navy. This was also when I started thinking I would someday like to be in Congress or some office where I could help people like FDR was doing in government. FDR was the first president or politician to use the radio for "Fireside Chats," and he had ways of speaking that made his listeners understand his positions.

I remember when FDR closed the banks and then re-opened them under new laws. He said that a boy who delivered newspapers and saved seven dollars, which he put in the bank, could no longer lose it because the bank was unsafe. He advocated for major changes in banking laws, and they were passed.

FDR was not raised in a poor family. Polio had left him highly disabled, but he responded to the 25 percent unemployment rate and other hardships of the recession with programs the country had never imagined adopting before that terrible depression. FDR embraced deficit government spending. It had really not been done before except to finance WWI, when $16 billion in bonds were sold. FDR asked and received the support from Congress, and

Me at the age of 4 near the house where I was born.

during the first 100 days they would approve almost any program he wanted to advocate. Congress passed several recovery programs to help with the food emergency, but as the depression continued, they continued to pass many other programs in a desperate attempt to "jump start" the free enterprise system.

One program that affected my family was the Civilian Conservation Corps (CCC). It was a program specifically designed for young men. The men received $25 per month in income, along with food and shelter. They lived in camps and the primary objective of their jobs was to improve the protections of natural resources. My older brother hitchhiked to California and joined the CCC. He was in a camp in Yosemite National Park. Boys were expected to send money home when they could. They had food and lodging and could live on $5 a month, so the other $20 should be sent home to help their families.

Another program for young men that was adopted later in the recession was the "NYA" National Youth Administration. The program was established in my hometown to build a town hall. The boys made cement blocks one at a time to form the walls. This was the first time anything like "cement blocks" had even been heard of in our town. I did not work on it, but I went to see it when it was completed. I saw the wonderful oak floor and immediately thought it would be a good place for dances. I rented it for $5 per night and could hire a six-piece orchestra for $5 to play dance music.

Another program that was established early in the recession to provide work for adults was the Works Program Administration (WPA). Anyone at any age could benefit from the program. They dug ditches in Packwood, leveled the land with spades and wheelbarrows near the school for a playground, and constructed a basement and gymnasium under the schoolhouse. Participants in that program included college graduates who were not able to find jobs. Numerous other work relief and natural resource programs were implemented and federally financed, but FDR also started programs like the National Assistant Act, under which local governments used matching funds and administrated the programs.

The New Deal also established programs directed at specific industries, such as the Agricultural Adjustment Act for farmers, the Federal Securities Act to protect investors, the Rural Electrification Act (REA) to extend electric service to rural areas, and the Farm Credit Act to help with mortgages on farms. The Social Security

Act was passed in 1935 with FDR's strong support and became a big issue in his 1936 campaign for re-election. It was the first big act based on accumulating funds to be available for use after retirement. It established the practice of using an actuarial valuation and was designed to keep retirees from needing emergency programs we had in the New Deal.

The New Deal programs were absolutely necessary and helped improve the lives of people around the country, but they did not end the depression. It was the Land Lease Program, in which we sent weapons and food to our future allies in Europe and our purchase for the war by piling up debt to pay for them, that gave the economy the huge demand that stopped the public critique of the free enterprise system and of our Constitutional form of government. Hatred for communism took place of that criticism after the war in what became known as McCarthyism. That was named for a Senator from Wisconsin who threw accusations at honorable citizens and dominated the news until a female senator from Maine, Senator Margaret Chase Smith, confronted him on the floor of the U.S. Senate.

New Deal programs to help farmers were especially important to us on the farm where my father could not secure enough from crop and pig sales to pay $5 per acre for rent. FDR appointed a well-known Iowan, Henry Wallace, as Secretary of Agriculture. In the Wallace's Farmer Magazine, Wallace had advocated what we thought at that time were radical programs.

Henry Wallace succeeded in getting a program passed called the Agriculture Adjustment Act (AAA) to destroy thousands or perhaps millions of cows and pigs to reduce supply and increase prices. He also got a program passed to plow under 10 million acres of cotton. Sale prices increased because there were fewer crops to sell.

Wallace was a strong advocate for research to learn how to increase efficiency and reduce costs per unit of production. He set up a swine research program near where he was working in D.C. It was in Beltsville, Maryland. During my service in Congress, I worked eight years to get it moved to Iowa, where I believed it should be and where the swine farms are. I secured the appropriation necessary for the building needed and it was built on the Iowa State Campus in 1994. The funds were also appropriated for facilities but opponents in Iowa government stopped it before the Swine Research Program was moved. I still believe it should be moved to Iowa where it could help solve problems such as reducing odors and diseases in swine farms.

There were numerous power and water projects implemented under FDR, such as the "TWA" Power and Water Control project that furnished electricity. There was pressure to limit the work per day to eight hours and time-and-a-half-pay for hours over eight.

Gold prices were established at $35 per ounce and stayed there until the Nixon Administration eliminated the price control in 1971. There was no limit on the prices of silver; the silver miners put a stop to that. This illustrated that the New Deal was not based on either economic theory or philosophy. FDR even changed his own positions, going away from the way he was raised, when he thought a different position would help the economy or better satisfy citizens. FDR received pressure to move to liberal positions based on using government as a tool, which changed his positions a lot in 1934 and 1935 to catch up with his followers.

I have been to the Iowa State Fair every year, except 1944, since 1934. In the several years before 1942, I was an exhibitor, sometimes in both the 4-H and the open class. I exhibited single ear and 10 ear samples of corn as well as vegetables in the open class in the Agriculture building. I exhibited chickens in the 4-H and the open class poultry buildings. One year I had the Grand Champion Trio. I have numerous ribbons from the Iowa State Fair and other shows. I sold roosters for hatchery flocks, and the prizes from numerous poultry shows, including the Minnesota and Illinois State Fairs, were good advertising. In those days, 4-H exhibitors had separate boys and girls buildings on the grounds where we could sleep, and our exhibits were on display for the entire fair.

One year, Bea, who would become my wife, her cousin from Tennessee, and their mothers came to the fair and were at the stage show. Bea and her cousin left their mothers and came to the 4-H building. Their cousin told them I was there. Bea had just celebrated her 16th birthday the month before. I went with them to see the various exhibits and explain why some had received prizes (e.g., the difference in a top Jersey cow and a top Hereford). We also looked at my Ag exhibits. It took about four hours, and their mothers were angry about having to wait for them. But when they said they had been looking at the exhibits with me, they weren't angry anymore.

The Iowa State fair was always important to me as a member of 4-H. I was also the Jefferson County President of the 4-H clubs one year. In 1942 and 1943, I just happened to be on furlough from the army and was able to spend at least one day during the fair. The only year I missed was 1944. I was deployed overseas when the fair was on.

1934 and 1936 were the driest and hottest years in my lifetime. We had no air conditioning, slept in the yard, and had bad crop failures in Iowa both years. There was a movement in the whole Midwest in those years to California. People loaded a pickup truck with their belongings and slept along the road on the way as they moved out to the west coast.

FDR had a very aggressive opponent in 1936. People were much more involved than usual in the political conversation, and I

Me and my pony Topsy, holding a pet raccoon in 1933. The raccoon
that would spread its legs and ride behind me when I rode bareback
on my pony. The neighboring children would often join together for
a pony ride along our dirt roads. My father had a cottontail rabbit
that would run along the outside of his yard fence that his rabbit dog
could not get through while it barked and pretended to get mad. We
had a squirrel that would cling to a tree about ten feet off the ground
barking at the St. Bernard dog while it pretended to be mad. Also we
had a Shetland sheep dog that went to the end of the lane when it was
time for the school bus and waited for the bus to come.

remember hearing those who were really concerned for FDR who
had been just as strongly for Hoover in 1928. This time it was not
a matter of religious or some other prejudice; it was a matter of
their economic existence. One big issue was Social Security. Social
Security was a major new step in using government for future
economic security. Unlike relief programs, it was an investment,
and we are so fortunate that it was set up to be actuarially sound

instead of depending on annual appropriations. In 1936, people were so happy in the grocery store when the radio reported that FDR received about 60 percent of the vote.

All seemed to be working out fairly well until the Supreme Court found some laws unconstitutional. FDR had appointed five justices but they did not have to rule the way the President proposed. The problem was so big and so important that FDR proposed increasing the number of justices so he could appoint more of them. It was called "packing the Court." If that had been approved, we would no longer be the first government in the world in which the temporary majority could not become a permanent majority. It was a major test of the U.S. form of Constitutional Government where the minority is protected.

There were other leaders in my early life who are also worthy of notice. One was John L. Lewis. He was a staunch Republican who had supported Hoover in 1932. He was a union leader in Clark County in southern Iowa, where there were coal mines. In 1934 and 1935 he ruled the United Mine Workers Union as an absolute Monarch and it gained national stature. But like FDR, over the period of the 1930s, he had to catch up with his followers.

Many people assumed unions were communist, but Lewis was anti-communist. Lewis was for labor organizations by each industry but there were large memberships for separate industries in the American Federation of Labor. They then separated into separate organizations. The CIO represented more of all factory workers while the AFL represented numerous mechanical trades. In 1936 a dispute that erupted in an auto plant, led to the CIO separating from the AFL. It was a major move, and in only about two years the United Auto workers increased from 88,000 to 400,000 members.

Coal mining was very important for all types of industry in the 1930s. Lewis became an activist leader, involved in not just mine worker's disputes and bargaining but others as well. He moved to Washington, D.C. and was there for many years.

In 1937, after the hot, dry, terrible year of 1936, things were so much better that even though there was still considerable national unemployment, it seemed by comparison as though recovery had finally been achieved. We also had much better crop yields. The Works Program Administration was reduced even though over one million citizens were still unemployed. When the payments into the Social Security Trust Fund were taken out of salaries and wages, some complained, but most still supported the Social Security program.

In the fall of 1937, the Stock Market collapsed and unemployment started to increase again. In 1938, unemployment was much worse, and FDR was blamed for assuming recovery and reducing government programs too soon. I remember some loafers at Saturday night gatherings on the street in front of the grocery stores blaming FDR and claiming free enterprise didn't work. Congress and FDR had to respond, and increased some of the programs like WPA again.

FDR made a brilliant speech on the radio just before the election. FDR said, "Martin, Barton, and Fish" were supporting his opponent, Wendell Wilke. The phrase was reported again and again on the street. Military build-up had done a lot for the economy in 1940.

By the time I started serving in Congress in 1959, most of the famous leaders in the 1930s were gone. But Claude Pepper of Florida was still there. He came to Iowa to a campaign rally. In 1938, several leaders quit and there was a massive gain for the Republicans. I was only 18, but I was interested in government, and I noticed that so many people who were much better off now than they were a few years ago were still dissatisfied instead of being thankful for the improvement.

In 1938, I was one year out of high school, and about the only way to make some money after farm work was done in the fall was hunting and trapping. I remember trapping a mink and its hide brought $5—a lot of money when there were no jobs available. But for that, I would have been much worse off. Also in that year I worked in the Nelson hatchery and built brooder houses for several people. A family near Grafton, in northern Iowa, heard I could be one to supervise building a barn. I hitchhiked up there and they hired me for $1 per day for 30 days with room and board. My parents took care of my baby chickens while I was gone. Jobs were still scarce. Some farm boys around Packwood hitchhiked to Michigan where dairy farmers were hiring for $30 per month with room and board.

In the late 1930s, the modern world was truly divided and would set on divergent paths. In Europe, Hitler was named Chancellor of Germany in January 1933 in the same month FDR became President of the U.S. In Germany, opposition parties were disbanded. The same could not occur in the U.S. under our Constitution. In Germany, cultural and religious choices were not a choice for individuals under the Hitler Nazi government. In the U.S., those choices were protected for all citizens, even including those with race, color, and religious differences. In Germany and Japan, and some other countries, those not in favor of the leadership were sent into slavery or murdered. That could not occur in the U.S. FDR was trying to end unemployment and economic hardships under the free enterprise system with government programs; in those other countries, they were using arms production and drafting able citizens into the armed forces to end unemployment.

Other events in the world affecting our future even more than our recession were just being hatched in 1939. Albert Einstein, in a letter to FDR on August 2, 1939, alerted the President that it was possible to develop an atomic bomb. Hitler was waging war in

Europe. One month later, on September 5, 1939, the U.S. declared that we would remain neutral and would not become involved in the war in Europe. In the U.S., in 1939, when I was living in Packwood, Iowa, we were strong isolationists. We had no idea the decision FDR made to develop the bomb that Einstein told him about, which would end a terrible war we would enter into only a few years later.

In 1939, decisions of importance to the future of the human species on this earth were being made by FDR, Hitler, the Emperor of Japan, and the Communist party in Russia. We were destined to go through six years of a horrible war before the free enterprise system under the U.S. Constitution and a post war alliance under NATO and the U.N. would win.

FDR secretly farmed out the research necessary to develop an atomic bomb. Experts and scientists at several institutions, including Iowa State University, were secretly involved. One day, in 1944, I was sitting in a tent in New Guinea, and a navigator on one of our crews was mad because he had to be there. He had advanced degrees in some sciences but was in the war as a navigator. He said, "We don't need to be here, they have an atomic bomb they could drop in the Japanese Harbor, and it would destroy so much of Japan that the war would be over." No one else in that tent had ever heard the words "atomic bomb" before; we thought he was ready for a Section 8 discharge for mental illness. Some of the research for the development of the bomb must have been at an institution he was at before he was enlisted.

This research was going on as a result of information given to FDR by an Israeli scientist. Hitler was killing and running Jewish people out of his "kingdom." Some were being welcomed to the U.S. That and many other examples resulted in the U.S. Free Enterprise System under our Constitution, winning over the dictatorships.

There have been and will continue to be disagreements about the New Deal and FDR's place in history, but everyone can agree that his presidency was one to be remembered for making an incomparable impact on the nation. He established that under our U.S. Constitution and capitalism, the U.S. government could and would have a major role in development. An outstanding example of this development is the interstate highway system.

FDR had proposed such a system as a works project. He proposed limiting access in the way it is limited now, but he also suggested that the Federal Government would condemn and own and sell land at a higher price at the accesses. That is how the system would be paid for.

The Eisenhower Administration said an interstate highway system was needed not for economic purposes but for defense purposes. Dwight D. Eisenhower, IKE, would have built it under contract as fast as possible, as individual projects are now let for the Defense Department. It would have been a five year project paid for by appropriations.

Lyndon B. Johnson was the Leader in the Senate and Sam Rayburn the Speaker of the House of Representatives. They provided the leadership to change it to a 20-year program paid for with a 7-cents-per-gallon gas tax.

Contractors were strong supporters of the Congressional 20-year program. They didn't want a big gear up for five years followed by a huge reduction in work as IKE had proposed. Also, the idea of users paying for it with a gas tax instead of with income tax was a popular one. The interstate system was completed in 22 years but now needs and receives more than the 7-cent tax that built it in costs to repair and extend it. The system is an outstanding example of something that would never have been accomplished under the theories of government existing before the New Deal Program.

two

Lessons From My Schooling & Service

Like most students in the ninth and tenth grades in the 1930s, I was already deciding what I would like to do as an adult. In the ninth grade, I decided I wanted to become a lawyer. The only way I might be able to do that was to work my way through Iowa State, become a 4-H leader, and earn enough to go to law school. I went to Ames and inquired at restaurants and other businesses but there was no way to work my way through college. The tuition was only $300 per semester in those days, but in the 1930s that was an impossible amount of money to earn while attending college.

So I worked in the Packwood area and saved a few dollars. My parents let me use their farm machinery and horses to farm 40 acres I had rented. I made good money shucking corn, and while most farm boys could not shuck 100 bushels per day, I could shuck as much as 150 bushels per day and scoop it into a crib. Using my own horses and wagon, I received $.05 per bushel. I acquired a DX gas station and ran it at night. I paid Ed Whitten $1.25 a day to run it in the daytime. By December 1941, I just about had enough to start my plan of working through Iowa State when Pearl Harbor occurred. My life was changed radically the night of December 7, 1941.

Up until Pearl Harbor occurred, my attitude, and almost everyone else's attitude in the Packwood area, was that we were strict isolationists. We knew Hitler was threatening to overrun Europe; we knew how evil he was. But we were protected by the oceans and Europe would just have to take care of its problems without our help.

I was in a theater in Fairfield, Iowa when the show was interrupted. It was announced that Japan had bombed Pearl Harbor. It was a Sunday night, December 7th. On Tuesday, I was in the old Federal Court House across the street from the Polk County Court House attempting to get into the Army Air Corps.

If I had already earned a college degree, I could have entered immediately but without a degree, I had to take an IQ test. I still don't know what the required score to pass was, but by 2 pm they said I had passed the test and I sat down with the recruiter. Just before I was going to sign up, he received a telegram saying the facilities were full and it would be six months before facilities would be available. I went home and started to sell property and turn over the farming I was doing to my father and uncle.

In January, my draft number came up. I was set to deploy on March 23, 1942—my birthday. I could have waited until an opening came in four months in the Air Corps, but I was ready to go. I sold my cattle and sheep and went into the regular army until an opening came available in the Air Corps.

I went overseas to Australia, New Guinea, and numerous islands in 1943 and came home May 15, 1945. When the war started and men left for service, a lot of bad judgments were passed on us, but in haste, all the young men went into the service. If they had a job,

Air Corps 1944.

they left it. If they had a car they sold it. Most wrongly assumed that their car would be worth less when they got out of the army because it would be older. But with no cars being manufactured during the war, they sold for a lot more.

IKE was the top General in both Africa and Europe and history will treat his leadership with great respect, but after an experience I had in 1946, I can't help but imagine what could have been and how it would have changed the U.S. When I built a house to sell to make some money while attending Syracuse University, I went to a lawyer for a legal opinion on the title to the lot. That lawyer, Clarence Ferch, happened to have been one of the three captains who were with Ike on a daily basis all during WWII in both Africa and Europe. Ferch said FDR and General Marshall had selected General Bradley to be the top general in Europe. But Bradley was still tied up in Italy when they were preparing for the invasion of Europe while Ike had finished in Africa. So Ike filled in handling the preparation for the Europe invasion until it became too late to change back to Bradley.

Just think what a difference it would have made in history if Stalin had not been so determined and FDR not been so stressed to move ahead. FDR was due on a ship to return to the U.S. and could not wait. But for that change, Bradley would probably have become President of the U.S. instead of IKE. John Foster Dulles would not have been Secretary of State either. Then, in the 1950s. Bradley might have responded the same way to IKE did to situations at hand.

Japan not only radically changed the countries who were in WWII when they executed Pearl Harbor, but they also became the only country against which the atomic bomb was ever used. The development of nuclear power, for both good and bad use, changed the world forever.

I returned to the U.S. in May of 1945. I was so weak and exhausted that I laid down on a bed in San Francisco on one day and did not wake up for 23 hours. I assumed at first that it was 11 hours later but found out I had missed my appointment for getting to Bea's graduation from Grinnell. I went down the street to a restaurant and ordered a steak. I had not had one for months. The clerk delivered it and I noticed people watching me eating that steak. It took a while for me to realize that the clerk must have given me his entire allotment for the month. Steaks at the time were not available in restaurants.

I finally got my physical, but I was told I must not fly home on an army plane. I had to take a train. I took a train to Marshalltown and found a bus that would take me to Grinnell. I arrived, and Bea met me at the bus station at 11 a.m. Her graduation was at 2 p.m. I could tell she was shocked at the way I looked when I got off the bus, but I was so glad to be there and attend her graduation. She had told me in letters for weeks how much she wanted me to be there.

I stood in line to meet the President of Grinnell, President Stevens, and he stopped and wanted to talk. He tried to recruit me to come to Grinnell. Although I was eligible for discharge, I intended to stay in the service until the war was over. Everyone assumed that the war would last two more years with great losses in Japan. It was well documented that Japanese soldiers would rather die than be captured. Until Truman dropped the atomic bomb, which we did not know existed, we expected at least two more years of battle. Truman ordered it dropped only because there were only more horrific alternatives.

Bea's parents took me home from Grinnell. I was so relieved. I assumed I would just spend my month furlough quietly between my home in Packwood and visiting Bea in Ottumwa, but I found myself suffering Malaria attacks. I had recurrent Malaria, but I knew how to get over an attack by taking Atriben tablets and keeping my temperature below 106 for two days. I had one attack while I was visiting Bea, and her mother took care of me. By the time my month furlough was up, I was doing fairly well. I drove to Los Angeles to make the choice of whether to be discharged or stay in. I chose to stay in and was sent to a base near Denver, Colorado. I had no idea the war would be over in three months.

In August, Truman ordered the bomb to be dropped, but the Japanese did not surrender. He ordered another one dropped. We now know it was a close call even after the bomb, but the opponents of the Japanese regime managed to gain control.

I was driving down the street in Denver when Truman announced they had surrendered and the war was over. People poured out of buildings, grabbing and kissing soldiers. I was driving a convertible and realized it was unsafe. I managed to turn down an alley and escape back to the base. It was late afternoon. When the base office opened at 8 a.m. the next morning, I was in the office requesting a discharge. The officer rolled his rolodex over. Everyone on the base was in the rolodex. He said, "You have more points than anyone else in the field. I am receiving permission to discharge two per day. I will prepare your papers while I wait for an order to discharge." I had to go to St Louis to be discharged.

It was the middle of the afternoon when I reached Columbia, Missouri. I had no intention of going to college there, but I stopped at the University of Missouri just to see what they had to offer. They recruited me. The President of the University asked to see me. I was the first veteran since the war was over to stop in the office. He offered to give me a semester of credit hours and let me take 23 hours per semester instead of the usual 16. I did not accept then, but after returning home and looking at two other possible Universities to attend, I accepted his offer and spent one year at Missouri before going on to Syracuse.

The war was over. The UN soon set up NATO and the allies handled peace with Germany and Japan much different than they had after WWI. It appeared that at last there would be no more wars. The world would be a loving place. No one thought we would soon suffer through more wars, more prejudice against specific groups of people, and such a need for good government under the great

U.S. Constitution. We simply were not prepared to be living in a world so over populated with humans that the balance of nature was so violated. We didn't know to expect new diseases and other consequences to the imbalance of nature due to overpopulation.

I was enrolled in classes in the Maxwell School of Citizenship at Syracuse University when Eleanor Roosevelt was Ambassador to the United Nations. She secured a worldwide unanimous agreement on human rights. No one else could have accomplished that. When she came to the Maxwell School and gave a speech, she personally met each of the school's 80 students. I have met leaders of countries, the Pope, and other important and powerful people and I have never been tongue-tied in their presence. But when I met Eleanor Roosevelt, I was so impressed by her that I could not talk. I thought she was the epitome of human service and the very picture of equality. I thought that the post WWII world would share her vision.

I soon found out that Eleanor Roosevelt and her desire for all people to be guaranteed human rights were the minority view in the world post WWII. It was not long before there arose extreme hatred toward individuals, McCarthyism, class warfare, religious prejudice, and lies about other religions. The 1950s and 1960s were destined to be tumultuous.

three

Lessons From the World Post-WWII

In 1946, I built a house by myself while I was attending Syracuse University. It cost $400 for the lot and $3600 to build the house. I sold it for $8,000. My wife Bea and I thought that with that profit and with the GI Bill and what I had saved we could make it through law school.

We had talked it over and she decided law school was the best way to prepare for the future, especially in view of my war-related health problems, including recurrent Malaria attacks.

Bea got better grades than I did in law school. Female lawyers were scarce and discriminated against at the time, and she was one of only three in law school and one of only three actively practicing in Des Moines after we graduated. An insurance company had offered both of us jobs, but I would receive $265 per month and Bea $165. We walked out and started our own private law practice instead. She had more clients walk in the door than I did. Most were women who had been discriminated against in court.

The house I built while attending college in Syracuse, NY.

I was at the University of Missouri in April of 1946. The President of the University called me and said Winston Churchill was coming to Fulton Missouri for a huge affair and that each University in Missouri could have two students in attendance. He asked if I wanted to be one of them, and of course I did! I think he called me because I had stopped at the University the day after the war ended and was in his office that day.

I was in attendance when Churchill and Truman came to Fulton on March 5, 1946. Churchill shocked us when he said that Russia was no longer our ally. The Cold War had started.

After Churchill came to Fulton and made that speech, it was apparent that post WWII was not the compassionate overpopulated world some assumed it would be. It was quickly becoming a divided world with more wars on its horizon. In the few months between the end of the war, in August 1945 and Churchill's speech in Fulton, Missouri in March 1946, it was obvious that the nation was headed into a different kind of war, called the Cold

War. Instead of being united by the hostility of Hitler, we were headed for a long period of distrust and competition with Russia and Communism as an ideology.

The survivors of WWII faced more problems than had been settled by the war itself. The end of WWII started the Cold War among the war victors. They now had to deal with questions such as how to deal with atomic bombs; do we have an occupation of Germany and Japan and by which countries? How long do we make them pay like we did following WWI, increasing continuing hatred? How do we limit the number of countries who own nuclear weapons? How do we prevent the problems that followed WWI and led to another war with weapons that could destroy thousands per day instead of the smaller numbers as in past wars?

There was a race by both Russians and the present NATO countries to occupy or keep others from occupying countries their armies were located in when the war ended. Some German leaders committed suicide, but others were tried and convicted. Nuremberg trials were arranged. Berlin was divided.

The Russians occupied the part where they had buried 7,500 Russian soldiers in a mass grave. I saw the grave in 1960. The Russian army had been killed in such numbers that they simply piled the bodies up and covered them with soil, making a huge mound in Berlin.

Some Japanese leaders were also convicted in post-war trials. Large numbers of Japanese leaders committed suicide because they believed it was the more honorable thing to do.

Both Germany and Japan were placed under military rule. MacArthur stayed in Japan and established a new government. To everyone's surprise, he used the Emperor as a tool in dealing with the population. Millions that might have committed suicide instead cooperated under the arrangement with the Emperor.

Japan under MacArthur used former Japanese leaders to help the country come rapidly under U.S rule. He rapidly established a Democratic government under a Constitution similar to ours that guaranteed human rights and personal freedom while outlawing war. The Emperor issued statements that the country would no longer would claim the Emperor was an absolute ruler or claim that the Japanese were a superior race to the rest of the world.

A United Nations Organization was formed, and it helped prevent the Cold War from turning more violent. Russia and other countries that might have turned violent used the United Nations to work through serious disagreements.

Russia wanted to regain the whole territory the Czars had occupied in Eastern Europe. They took Poland and the Baltic States immediately. Stalin was installing a Communist Union that combined an economic and military block. The U.S., on the other hand, had a policy of returning countries to independent states. The U.S. had greatly reduced the forces we had in Europe at the end of the war in May 1945. The Soviets attempt to bully a few countries in the old Czar territory, but even though they failed, they still formed a large Soviet Union.

The Cold War did, however, help to make us even more friendly and co-operative with the pre-war giant Germany. The allies had, in 1943, agreed to divide Germany into three zones, but now the movement to make all of Germany an ally and partner with others in Eastern Europe was sure to occur. While Stalin was incorporating as much as he could into the Soviet Union, the U.S. and Britain were actively pursuing a policy of containment, an even more important close co-operation, and no longer engaging in wars over borders. The Truman Doctrine promised aid to any country resisting the loss of democratic freedom. The giant question in the coming struggle was who would have access to the new nuclear weapons.

The Smith family upon graduating Law School.

The Western Powers set up the North Atlantic Treaty Organization (NATO), which would prove to be extremely important because of the Soviet threat. Germany was admitted to NATO in 1955.

In the Cold War period following WWII, there was a huge backlog of demand in the economy. It seemed that almost everything was in short supply, partly from lack of production (such as in automobiles) during the war and partly to satisfy the huge return of veterans and the increase in families. There was a need for triple the number of buildings on college campuses to satisfy the housing need for returning veterans attending school on the GI bill.

There was also a big move with increased international transportation equipment toward globalization of the world economy. I remember an International Agreement decreasing the number of Tariffs was signed by many countries in 1947, while I was at Syracuse University, and that had a very limited effect.

Eleanor Roosevelt was the Ambassador to the United Nations and she obtained unanimous agreement for a Human Rights Proclamation. The world could agree on her Resolution on Human Rights, but there was no worldwide agreement on Trade Tariffs.

Though most of the U.S. population was fed up with the war, we still became involved militarily in the Cold War period, and it wasn't a political divide. In 1947, when Truman was President, we became involved in Greece. A war then broke out in Korea. Communists wanted to acquire control of it. Harry Truman appointed General MacArthur to handle the military. He did a brilliant job of making a surprise invasion up north. The U.S. Allied Forces moved north rapidly. President Truman's war cabinet in Washington ordered MacArthur not to force North Korean soldiers up to the border and into China. MacArthur disobeyed his orders. China responded by entering the war and driving the U.S. allies south. Truman fired MacArthur for disobeying orders, and he was forced to retire to the U.S. for the first time since before WWII. The Chinese drove the U.S. allies south and came to a halt where it still is at the demilitarized zone (DMZ). There still is no treaty ending the war and no settled division line. I think North and South Korean want and need to join together again, but China will not agree to that.

Stalin was a very important figure in World History and an extreme and, apparently, almost dictator leader, though Russia has a Communist Party Committee. He died in 1953. Other leaders were appointed, and in 1956 Nikita Khrushchev emerged as a less extreme leader. The world was shocked to hear Khruschev denounce Stalin's leadership, but the Cold War was still on, and he was removed after the Cuba Crisis. I was in Congress by that time.

Though there was a split among Republicans between the Taft part of the Republican Party and the majority, both Republicans and Democrats in government positions were in agreement relative to Korea. During the Eisenhower Administration, we were also involved militarily in Iran and Lebanon, and the Eisenhower Doctrine was proclaimed during that time, which committed us to oppose any further spread of Communism. That was an important Doctrine and it was widely agreed to.

While a tug of war was going on in Europe between Russia and the other allies from WWII, Russia was moving in Asia. A war broke out in Korea between what became a Communist North and a South protected by U.S. forces. Merely having an alliance with the U.S. had not proven to be enough to keep countries in the Mideast safe from Communism, and hatred for Communism became a tool used for dividing Americans. McCarthism in defensive form was prevalent for many years.

The U.S. had a monopoly on the atom bomb in 1945. The question some asked was, should the U.S. exercise whatever military power we need to keep all others from acquiring the ability to produce one? Though in the long run it would probably have saved the world from death, it might have also resulted in immediate death of U.S. citizens. The U.S. population was in no way willing to become involved in another war, even if we knew it would prevent Russia from obtaining this horrible weapon. Russia ended our monopoly in 1949 when they succeeded in developing the bomb. Then the race was on to see who could acquire and have available for delivery the most missiles. It also finally led to the confrontation in Cuba in 1962 and numerous problems in other countries as others secured access to the secrets needed to make the

Senator Kennedy and Congressman Smith in 1960.

bomb. Outlandish production and accumulation of bombs did not end between the U.S. and Russia until in the 1970s when verifiable agreements were finally made and the number in the U.S. and in Russian storage were actually reduced.

There is no doubt in my mind that we are so fortunate to have NATO and such a small probability of another war breaking out in Eastern Europe. NATO and the U.N. were a huge gain for peace in our century. We still have veterans in the country, thousands upon thousands, who lived through these wars and suffer because of old injuries and mental trauma.

The Japanese had used their ingenuity and resources in between the wars to extend a huge empire all the way from China and Western Russia and including islands bordering Australia. Their Empire included countries and islands that were well advanced in technology and those that were a thousand years behind. As the U.S. took responsibility for Japan's protection from invasion, they were following WWII in a position to advance in manufacturing technology at an extremely fast rate. Japan became recognized as highly competitive in industry with any competitor worldwide. They became a competitor with the U.S. in the economic balance of power while the U.S. was protecting them militarily.

With the successful establishment of NATO and the U.S. relationship with Japan both heeding great success, both former enemies, Germany and Japan, have become super economic powers in the World and great allies to the U.S. since the conclusion of the war. Both Japan and Germany were in shambles at the end of WWII, and their economies even worse than the U.S. economy was in 1930. With war no longer an objective to secure territory, and with our help, both became Capitalist bulwarks and joined the U.S. in building the greatest ever period for development and economic prosperity. Output in Japan, Germany, and the U.S. in the post war years grew at around 10 percent. Education was recognized in all three countries and most of the world as being extremely important, and this soon led to the development of substitutes for personal labor. Robots, computers, and chemicals were so important to our economies but also lead to unemployment problems in a free enterprise economy.

It was clear that the oceans no longer separated the world in conflicts that caused war. Some diplomatic doctrines and organizations were formed. There was the Truman Doctrine, the Treaty Organization, and the Marshall Plan. They were important, resulting in Germany being a partner in a new European Union for economic purposes and NATO for military protection. Russia shocked us when they incorporated countries they occupied into the Soviet Union and treated them as part of one big country.

In 1947 and 1948, Poland, Hungary, Czechoslovakia, Bulgaria, Romania, and Yugoslavia became part the Soviet Empire. I was in those very states just three weeks before they broke away from the Soviet Union, signaling the collapse of the union in 1989. I was in Hungary serving as Chairman of the State Department Committee on Appropriations. In 1989, Hungary was planning to break away from the Soviet Union. The Communists in Hungary, or the ones who were supposed to be loyal to Moscow, were part of the group planning the breakaway. I learned in those other countries, especially Romania and Czechoslovakia, that they were waiting on Hungary to make the first move, and that move occurred three weeks later.

The years in which Britain was involved in other wars gave British-occupied India an opportunity to experiment with having their own government instead of being controlled by the Europeans. The League of Nations had approved separating it into two countries, India and Pakistan, so as to prevent the many problems stemming from religious differences in those territories. India had been important trading partners for Britain, but they were granted independence in 1947. They had the capacity and did in fact become a more and more important country in trade and immigration problems with the U.S.

Many countries in Asia and Africa became independent and had problems establishing a government we would prefer they establish. Many of these difficulties still existed to some extent at the beginning of the 21st century.

Britain and France had also been active in the Middle East between World Wars. Syria, Lebanon, Jordan, Libya, Egypt, and other countries moved toward independence in the period immediately following the war. The necessity for doing something big for the Jewish population that had been treated so horribly by Germany under Hitler led to a big controversy. Harry Truman was criticized when he strongly supported re-establishing a new country for the Jewish people from where they had been run out in the ancient past. He was heavily criticized but successful, and Israel was recognized by the new United Nations Organization. There was, however, and has been ever since, problems involving where the boundaries should be drawn. When boundaries were set for the new Israel, there was no way to satisfy everyone, including those who occupied parts of the area since the ancient days when the Israelis were run out. In the end, boundaries were set according to where the occupiers before 1948 had been. For example, Britain had occupied the East of the Sea of Galilee on one side but the other side had only a narrow area for the road. That became the border with Syria, though neither side liked it. The boundary lines have caused problems ever since.

Egypt and Syria had close relationships with the Soviet Union in the 1960s, including in military advice and weapons. They hoped to use that relationship to remove Israel from the area, but that led the U.S. to provide strong military assistance to Israel. This whole area has been at war on some level ever since.

four

Lessons About Discrimination & Communism

One major change resulting from the great depression and the New Deal was the change in citizens' attitudes toward people of different origin, religion, and circumstances. I noticed that since the New Deal and WWII, people were far less compassionate and far more selfish toward others than they were during the hardships I witnessed as an Iowa teenager during the depression. I think the origin of the major movements under Lyndon B. Johnson to eliminate or at least reduce discrimination was in the hardship we saw others suffer during the depression. Women were given the right to vote in 1920, but they were discriminated against in employment and wages until long after the depression and WWII—and even still today. The attitudes of American and Western World citizens in time of depression and in time of war re more valuable in important ways. We certainly don't want to be living in either state, but we should learn something by observing the way in which during the depression, people helped one another. Bums walked down the roads in Iowa and stopped to sleep in our barn; they walked on the dark streets in Packwood; they were hungry but they did not break into the grocery store to steal food. We did not keep our doors locked at night when strangers were sleeping in the barn; we didn't feel the necessity to do so. We shared food with complete strangers because we knew their hunger was not their fault. People who were more discriminatory toward those with differing religions, races, etc. still wanted to help those people secure food and shelter.

In times of war, women had jobs that they were denied or paid less per hour for after the war ended. In wartime, after December 8, 1941, people like me who were once isolationists became the opposite—simply due to the fact that Japan had bombed Pearl Harbor.

A whole population of a country can be changed by either mass economic or mass safety concerns. Unfortunately being more fortunate or safer has, in both cases, affected the population of a whole in a negative way.

When LBJ was President, the world was very unpleasant from the standpoint of war, but it was vastly more successful and important than any other in helping the free enterprise system become more successful than any other in providing economic opportunity. Under Medicare, Medicaid, and other programs, Federal programs made states partners, whether they wanted to be or not. In this last century, I think that although FDR faced much greater problems, LBJ will be considered the most successful President in economic leadership and Nixon the most successful in foreign affairs.

Discrimination was a difficult topic that LBJ faced. Race relations were especially bad in some states, but discrimination extended beyond race to ethnicity, sexual orientation, and other differences. The different countries people in certain communities came from resulted in discrimination. When immigrants moved

Smith with LBJ in the oval office.

west in the 1800s, they settled in communities that were different in religion and other ways than the community next door. It was my generation that mixed it up. In the 1930s, it was a popular happening for teenagers in one community to have a girl or boyfriend in another community. When settlers moved west, they tended to start cities in the upper fork of two rivers. Native Americans had done the same thing. They could use the rivers and the highest land and avoid having floods destroy their cities. Everyone assumed that if there had never been a flood on a piece of land along the river, there never would be. By the 1960s, floods were occurring in many cities and there was a period when major dams were built all over the country, both for electric power production and the safety of infrastructure from flooding. Now it is apparent to almost anyone that both cities on rivers and cities near ocean coasts are going to be at great risk of flooding and other natural disasters with the negative effects of climate change.

Under Nixon, Kissinger negotiated with both the Chinese and Russian leadership and greatly reduced tension while helping both countries. For example, Kissinger's negotiations resulted in the reduction of the huge supply of atomic weapons both Russia and the U.S. had. Though we are under constant risk and fear that one person or a group will cause huge human loss with the use of an atomic weapon, we are safer now than ever before from a war emerging over border protection among the whole group of countries in NATO. Establishing NATO was an enormous gain for protections against the outbreak of another world war.

Russia under Communism used forced labor. They made sure everyone worked. As late as 1961, when I was on an Education Exchange in Russia, I saw an example of Communism when I was on a trip there. In a field, they were preparing for planting corn, a large tractor was disking in a huge field, and hundreds of women were preparing the same fields with hoes. The alternatives to our free enterprise system under the U.S. Constitution would have been much worse, but in bad economic times in the U.S. when they persisted, some adults on a Saturday night gathering said that they would choose some alternative.

In 1959, Roswell Garst of Iowa was engaging in discussions with Soviet leaders concerning agricultural matters, which I discovered they had a heightened interest in. When I was in Congress in 1959, I received a call from the Soviet Ambassador. Even talking to him was enough to label me a Communist sympathizer and some kind of an enemy in a country that propelled hatred toward the Communists that existed in the U.S. But I took the call regardless. The Ambassador's office said the Ambassador had an invitation to attend a meeting at Simpson College and wanted to know if I thought it was safe to go. Someone from the Russian Government had attended a meeting in California and caused a big ruckus. I said he would be safe, and that if Simpson College wanted him to come, I would ask my personal friend, the Polk County Sheriff, to see that he was delivered safely.

I did not know it then, but the Ambassador was setting up a dry run before deciding whether to accept an invitation from Roswell Garst for Khrushchev to visit the Garst farm. There were people in the U.S. who wanted to show they were more anti-communist than others, and there were three or four well financed anti-communist organizations nationwide. One of them was known as the John Birch Society. They claimed that my accepting a chance to help Simpson College secure the Communist Party Speaker as proof that I must be associated with the Russian Communists. The group sent three activists to Des Moines, opened a bookstore, and started campaigning against me. I responded by taking statements and questions from them in public meetings and ridiculing what they were doing. At a meeting with the Des Moines Chamber of Commerce, they said I should not be in favor of building Red Rock Dam because there was no money to pay for it. I responded by asking the Chamber to have a big thank you party for those contractors who were building such a valuable asset for future generations without receiving any money for the work.

The three new members of the John Birch Society remained my most active opponents, especially in the 1962 election. They were heavily financed and spewed hatred and accusations against other people, and they including some members of Congress such as Joe McCarthy and Nixon, when he first came to Congress. These activities seemed to spring up and exist when times were good, which was just the opposite of the compassionate way people acted back in the deep depression when times were so bad for almost everyone. But hatred for Communism helped drive European countries, including Germany, into a very effective NATO alliance. The result of NATO was that there has been no war between those European Nations since 1945, the longest period in modern history. I hope that peace will last forever. It is a lesson to be learned and a sad fact to be acknowledged that humans seem to be compassionate for one another or whole groups only when they have an enemy to join forces against.

A very important event occurred when women were given the right to vote in the first year of my century of life. My mother and father voted in every election. I did not realize how important an event it was that women gained the right to vote was until I was in politics myself. We used women to get men to vote in Polk County in the 1950s. We made an effort to get women, most of whom did not have jobs, to vote in the day time and then asked them to urge their husbands to vote when they came home from work. Women exercising the right to vote was extremely important not just from a human rights standpoint but also because they did not vote exactly as men did and that difference in voting trends makes a huge difference since women numbered greater than men in the country. I concluded during the 40 elections I was on the ballot that at least 5 percent of married women not only vote different from their husbands but also, rather than cause an unpleasant argument, don't tell him they are voting for different candidates. This is especially true in elections where there are hot button issues affecting women at the forefront of conversation.

five

Lessons From The Vietnam War

After WWI, European countries had made themselves protectorates of some countries in Asia and virtually all of Africa. They gave themselves favorable trade deals with those countries and could do so because those countries either did not have ships or the ability to protect their ships. But following WWII, both France and Britain were abandoning those connections. That was especially the case for France. France was leaving Vietnam, Laos, Cambodia, and the area it was assumed would be a target of the Communists. It also was assumed that Russia was the big giant gorilla that wanted to become the dominant power in the world and was moving to that position in that Asian area.

Eisenhower's Secretary of State was John Foster Dulles. He went into countries France was leaving and arranged treaties between those countries the U.S. in order to protect them. He just assumed that no one, including Communists, would dare touch a country the powerful U.S. was protecting.

Secretary Dulles came to Des Moines and attended a political meeting in the Fort Des Moines Hotel. I slipped into the back and listened to his talk. Dulles thought the event of the U.S. signing those treaties was almost equal of the ceremony in which MacArthur signed the big treaty with Japan. He could not understand why the media had not treated it as a salvific act of protecting a whole chunk of Asia from Communism.

It did not prevent political and military pressures in those countries. When the Viet Cong tried to take over Vietnam, it was assumed that if the country was not protected, other Asian countries, including the balance of Korea, would follow. So the U.S. became involved with "advisors," and the situation slowly escalated into war. No one in the U.S. wanted a war in Vietnam, but we feared that failure to defend our treaty obligations would lead to the loss of other countries and even endanger Japan. There was no question that we would become heavily involved if Japan was attacked; our treaty left them without enough defense in either army or navy to defend themselves.

There was a period of several years when the Eisenhower, Kennedy, and Johnston Administrations tried to arrange agreements to prevent military activity, but they always failed. The Vietnam War was terrible and no one wanted it, but we will never be sure what the alternative would have been had we suddenly pulled out.

Vietnam is one of several Asian countries on the other side of the globe that has been in or in threat of war since WWII. Both the older generation that lived for decades during that war and the younger generation alike for the most part criticize the government for entering the war and for executing it in the way it was executed. The Vietnam war has become a major blemish on the country's history for my generation but it involved far more than the just period during which we were at war in Vietnam.

General LeMay handing Smith a certificate. LeMay was the
top general at the Pentagon at the time.

The French and others were for several generations using Asian
countries as a resource for rice and other products, and they had
found ways to do so at the expense of the natives of those countries.
All of our Presidents from Truman through Nixon were involved in
the Vietnam problem, and they felt they must be involved in order
to avoid some other worse outcome.

The day in 1946 when I sat in that crowd listening to Churchill
in Fulton, Missouri was the day my generation began to be
involved in Vietnam a way that would lead to the deaths of 47,000
U.S. soldiers. Churchill told us that Russia was bent on spreading
Communism by military force. Asian countries would not be
exempt. Russia has islands near their borders in Northern Japan
and wanted to take them for Communism. We were obligated to
protect Japan because we denied the country a substantial army
and navy as part of our war settlement.

Smith talks with American servicemen at an advance
outpost in Cambodia during the Vietnam War.

Truman and Eisenhower, without significant opposition
in either political party in Congress, subscribed to the Domino
Theory. Under the Domino Theory, it was believed that if Vietnam
could be forced to accept a Communist Government associated
with Russia, other Asian Countries would follow suit. IKE only
temporarily declared an end to involvement in 1955, but a leader
named Diem came into power in 1956 which caused IKE to reverse
his declaration. IKE thought helping Diem was the thing to do
to prevent the Communists from occupying Vietnam. IKE, JFK,
LBJ, and Nixon all had good reason to believe a Vietnamese leader
would be able to give the Vietnamese people the government they
wanted, but one after another leader disappointed them.

Christmas Card photo with LBJ.

It is hard for U.S. citizens who did not live in the 1950s and 1960s to understand how strongly virtually everyone in the U.S. considered a Communist conspiracy a real, mounting threat. It was a threat also that we all believed truly warranted sending military help to those who sought independence in Vietnam to keep it free of Communism. The Viet Cong did not have troops organized in rifle companies and battalions. They were spread out and were using civilians who were not in uniform. Our response had to be entirely different than it was in WWII and Korea, so JFK used what were called "advisors" to help the locals on our side with both hardware and advice. The objective, and the challenge, was to "Save Vietnam" and establish a government that could be trusted to be remain anti-Communist.

The first death of U.S. advisers occurred in 1962, but by the time JFK was assassinated we had 11,200 "advisers" in Vietnam and were developing a whole new way to fight a war. To expose opponents carrying in arms, the U.S. even used agent orange to destroy a strip of forest. I was going to meetings of veterans held in Congress with Senator Barry Goldwater as the leader to receive reports. One day, the top U.S. General came to the meeting and reported they had used a chemical to in attempt to kill a strip of forest two days before, but that it didn't work. In fact, he said, it acted like a fertilizer. Neither he nor anyone else at the meeting besides me knew that was the way the chemical worked. The leaves expand until the 3rd or 4th day, when they would explode and die. The other people in the meeting had not taken the course on chemicals at West Point. I was the only one in that veterans meeting who knew how Agent Orange worked. Not even the leader in the Pentagon knew.

I was the ranking member appointed to the only official Congressional Committee formed to secure information for Congress on the conduct of the war in Vietnam. We traveled in helicopters high above the ground over all four zones. The helicopters flying low to pick up injured Americans were in danger of approaching Viet Cong who hid in the grass or rice and shot them down.

We were there shortly after our troops went into Parrots Bank in Cambodia—a small area sticking up into Vietnam that the Viet Cong had been using as their warehouse for arms. There was a stack of automatic rifles that had been carried down from the North one or two at a time. The pile was a city block long, 30 feet tall, and 200 feet wide. The General gave me one to bring back to the states, and I took it to the Museum at Camp Dodge where it was put on display.

Arriving on a helicopter in Vietnam in 1971.

Vietnam was a terrible war. No one really wanted the U.S. to be there, but we felt like it was a unfortunate necessity. Public Television did a documentary on it, but few people who still criticize the Presidents, including Truman, IKE, JFK, LBJ and Nixon, for not keeping the U.S. out of the war don't realize how much pressure they were under to stay until they had an assurance that the Vietnamese people would not be forced into a Communist camp. To understand the Vietnam War, people need to look back at the entire history of the conflict, from 1920 through the Nixon period.

The U.S. continued during the period from Eisenhower to Carter to be heavily involved in the Vietnam war. All leaders in Congress wanted to find a satisfactory way for it to end. We wanted out, but there were deep divisions in opinion on how to do that. Some wanted to just leave, even though it would violate agreements made by the Eisenhower Administration to keep Vietnam from falling to the Communists. Attempts in the U.S. at making agreements that it be divided or be independent were rebuffed. There was great fear, for good reason, that violating our agreement with the Vietnam government would encourage the Communists to move to take over other countries with whom Dulles had negotiated similar agreements. There was a real fear in our intelligence services (and it was bi-partisan) that if we did not find a way out other than by breaking our agreement, it could even get us into a war under our obligation to Japan, which had no army or navy and depended on the U.S. completely. We were at the height of fear that Communism would spread to the whole Pacific area.

We finally did withdraw in the worst way because we couldn't do otherwise, but it did not result in the way we feared most. We still do not know how close we came to the worst results.

Far too many people dwell on a relatively small part of the history of the Vietnam pre-war and war period and reach conclusions they would not reach if they knew the whole story. There is no room in this brief summary of my century for such a history, but I will set forth a brief outline of important events involving the Vietnam War:

1. France became the protectorate of Vietnam and some other Asian countries before and after WWI.

2. Japan temporarily occupied it in WWII.

3. France abandoned it in about 1956.

4. The Eisenhower Administration, with John Foster Dulles as Secretary of State, made the U.S. responsible for Vietnam's safety thinking that would save the

country from Communism and no one would oppose U.S. authority. But they did.

5. The Gulf of Tonkin Resolution delegated the right to go to war to prevent Vietnam from becoming Communist and encouraged China and Russia to do the same thing in other Asian countries.

6. The U.S. draft laws, which were changed more than once, did not make all young men equally required to go to war.

7. Several attempts were made by both LBJ and Nixon to end the war without encouraging the Communists to move on other countries. They were rebuffed.

8. We had an obligation to defend the territory Japan surrendered to us because we denied WWII Japan of having an adequate army and navy to fight a war.

I was a member of the only Congressional Committee that went to Vietnam for 15 days in 1971 to seek information on how to proceed. We recommended withdrawing 10 days at a time, under certain conditions, but our recommendation was not accepted.

The whole story about Vietnam and other wars since need to be documented here. We should also note that the generation of U.S. citizens under the age of 35 did not live during those wars. For the first time in history, members of the younger generation are more numerous than the older generations. Also, younger generations have lived in a world with such a different perspective about many questions affecting our country. War had a huge impact on my generation in many ways, with both good and bad results.

six

Lessons From Life as a Lawyer and Congressman

In 1948, during Bea's and my second year of law school, one of our friends said a relative of his did not feel like her farm manager was doing a very good job. He asked me to let her show me her records. She was right. Her farm manager was just keeping her books and charging a percentage of her income for doing so, at her request, I became her farm manager.

Within two or three weeks, four or five of her widowed friends came to me with the same problem from the same Farm Management Company. I formed my own farm management corporation, The Iowa Farm Management Company, and registered the company name. So in addition to going to law school, I was now managing farms. I continued managing those farms, and added several more of them to my company, until I was elected to Congress in 1958.

The Pittsburg Des Moines Steel Company, which sold and still sells steel parts for construction jobs asked me to find them a suitable place to move to. They were in south downtown Des Moines and needed a much larger place. They gave me all the requirements, and I found a farm on Hickman Avenue with the drainage, railroad and highway access, and everything else they needed. They are still located there to this day. At that time they moved there, they were located in the country, but with the way Des Moines has expanded, they are now only part way into the developed area of the city.

Since I had helped them in their location search, they also sought my help in settling wage negotiations and in setting up a retirement plan.

I was called into another negotiation with the Construction Trade and other employers. I realized that a retirement plan would be the answer to their problem. The problem was that the defined benefit retirement plans had only been approved for employees of a singular employer. We needed a plan that would allow employees to qualify for retirement while working for several employers over the entire period of employment. The plan I came up with would fix the problem they were having because the contribution would be worth the full amount to the employees but also deducted from the employer's taxes.

The employers' attorneys said the IRS would never approve my plan, but I thought I could create one that would qualify. The employees said they would take the chance. We submitted the plan to IRS, and to every ones surprise, they approved it in a matter of only about three weeks. That was the first multi-employer defined benefit plan approved in the U.S.

A National Tax Publication called me and sought information on the plan I had implemented for Construction Trade. I told them I sold my time, and they readily purchased eight hours. I showed them the details. I could have arranged for a highly profitable arrangement, but I foolishly did not realize what could occur from our discussion. They published my plan nationwide, and in a matter of a few weeks, Multi-employer Defined Benefit Plans were being established throughout the U.S.

While not all of the plans that came from my basic structure are without issue, one outstanding example is the IPERS retirement plan for retirees in the State of Iowa. In 1992, IPERS secured an actuarial evaluation that justified levels of benefits that exceeded what was "sound." Since that time, existing retirees have received over $5 Billion more out of the reserve fund than was actuarially sound. The same has occurred in most states and a large percentage of industries.

I was the National President of the Young Democrats in 1953 and 1954. There were 300,000 members of the Young Democrats, and most were veterans of WWII. I was also an Adlai Stevenson supporter. I went to his farm home west of Chicago one morning to meet with him and his Executive Secretary, who was also an official in the National Young Democrats. Adlai's home was a nice small house on the knoll with cheviot sheep in a large front yard. He was in a meeting when I arrived, so I waited until the participants left. One of them was Jack Arvey, the boss in Chicago. I asked my friend what they had been discussing, and he said, "They just selected the next Mayor of Chicago, an alderman named Richard Daley." Richard Daley had not been in the meeting, but we sure heard a lot about him for many years after that. I thought it was interesting that so few been part of the selection process. Daley was re-elected for many years after that.

When Adlai Stevenson was running for President in 1952, he came to the Plowing Match in Jasper County, which was about 20 miles east of our farm. Bea made lunch and we met him at the airport in Des Moines and drove him to the Match, eating the lunch on the way. We had a white peach tree that produced beautiful sweet peaches. She put some in a small jar for dessert. While he was eating the main lunch, Stevenson ate a spoonful of the fruit, put the rest of the lunch down, and finished the peaches. He said they were the best he had ever eaten.

When I was in Congress, I was hospitalized with a seizure due to re-current Malaria. While there, they told me I was eligible for a 30 percent veterans disability. I did not take it. I was able to handle my job in Congress despite my health issue and thought that was not necessary. Since I was discharged, I have accepted a 10 percent eligibility, which I have kept so I could be eligible to go to veterans hospitals if I needed to. I have not been in a veterans hospital since I was in law school, but there are tens of thousands who desperately need to have access to the VA hospitals around the country. While we appreciate the gains we enjoy from establishing NATO and in the way we handle foreign entanglements, we will be paying for those wars for a long time both financially and in the health of our veteran citizens. It is the obligation of our army to keep us as safe as possible while also continuing to pay for the past.

I have had some unique experiences with world leaders, such as the one where Gorbachev, when he was still the head of the Soviet Department of Agriculture, quizzed me at length about how to increase meat production from the national herd of reindeer. So I helped the future leader of the Soviet Union increase meat production. But perhaps an experience more unique is the one I had with the leader of the free world, President Lyndon Johnson in Des Moines, Iowa on October 8, 1964.

President Johnson was on a very short campaign stop in Des Moines. I had joined him at a stop in Indiana and had briefed him on the way to Des Moines. We departed Air Force One at the Des Moines Airport and headed for the white house limousine which had arrived on another plane. On the way he shook hands with a hundred people who stood along the fence. We then headed down Fleur Drive waving to thousands along the edge of the road.

When we arrived just north of Bell Avenue where there are no places for a crowd to stand along the street. The President suddenly asked, "Neal, do you know where I can find a good Lanrace Boar?" I said, "I do, I just purchased some sows from a Landrace Breeder and he had an excellent Landrace Boar for sale."

LBJ immediately put me on his car telephone making a purchase of the boar and also arranging with his farm manager in Texas to handle the delivery and paper work.

All of that was completed by the time we arrived on 5th Street downtown Des Moines, at that point he stopped the limousine, jumped out and shook hands with the crowd for several minutes and the proceed on to the rally on the west lawn of the capitol. I had just helped the leader of the free world acquire a Landrace Boar.

Although I was with LBJ in person and on the telephone many times after that, he never again mentioned that Landrace Boar.

That was in the 44th year of my century. No world leader today in the 98th year of my century could dare expose himself to danger so many times, acquire a boar, and speak to 130,000 people who were not searched for weapons and then depart in the 3 hour period.

I did a lot of traveling in the same plane that was usually assigned for the 15 day trips I went on, from 1970 to 1994, as chairman of an appropriations sub-committee in the House, where all appropriations begin. When a bill is signed by the President, the only name on the bill is the Chair of the sub-committee in the House. That meant that my name is the only one besides the President's on dozens of bills. I met with top leaders in the many countries I traveled to. The Deputy U.S. Secretary of State for Administration was one of six or eight others who travelled with me.

That 1970 to 1994 period was an extremely active period in which adverse changes were occurring in many countries of the world that could have been avoided had they had enforced a

Secretary of State Kissinger.

Constitution like ours. In too many countries, when one person or a specific group takes the reins of government, they use the army to prevent some other group from gaining leadership, become rich through dishonesty, and move government money to a foreign country for safe keeping.

I was in Venzuela on the day when, for the first time in history, a newly elected government group was allowed to take over the Venezuelan government. Right up to the last minute, we expected that the army would be used to prevent the transition. But the very group that was elected then did not let another election remove them from office. They ended up being the worst government to rule in South America. They could have been an example of free election, but if a country does not have all the rights we enjoy through a Constitution, and enforced by a Supreme Court and the legislative limitations, that government can instead become corrupt.

We should be making a far greater effort to convince leaders in those countries that they should follow the example of the founders of our country. I also think we should be making a far greater effort to promote trade between the countries in South and Central America. We would all experience gain if we would trade surpluses for shortages in all these countries, and citizens in each country would be better off in that situation if they stayed in their native country instead of illegally immigrating to the U.S.

In the 80 countries I traveled to in order to oversee the U.S. State Department and Commerce Departments representation in those countries, we almost always found ways to either save money or improve the operation. The U.S Secretary of State also travels a great deal to examine economic, military, diplomatic, and other matters. The Secretary of State under Nixon, Ford, Reagan, and Bush 41 was always a Republican, while the majority of the committee I chaired were Democrats, but in those days, that was a non-issue. I also often met with the Secretary of State in my private office. When sensitive matters came up, I met in a private office or a debugged room in the Capital with Henry Kissinger, George Shultz, Colin Powell, James Baker, and Lawrence Eagleburger. I had great respect for all of them and have flattering letters that I received from each one of them. One time I met Secretary Baker at midnight when he arrived from one trip and was turning around to start on a new trip with a new staff the next day. One time, I was not able to agree with a Secretary of State due to the way an Assistant Secretary of State was performing, and she was fired as a result of me sharing my opinion with him.

I was in Japan in a research institution where they built an engine that a human touched at only six stations. At each place,

1971 with Deng Xiaoping when he was the
paramount leader of China.

a computer checked to see if the human had made a mistake. It cost more to build that engine than it cost for engines built in U.S. factories, but it was also a superior product. For example, the bolts holding the head on were tightened precisely the same tightness, which resulted in the gasket lasting longer. Technology has constantly replaced middle-to-low income workers and will continue to do so.

Before 1949, China was being led by Chiang Kai-Shek. China did not become Communist until 1949. For the three years before 1949, Stalin supported Mao, who wanted a Communist China. Until Henry Kissinger, under President Nixon, arranged for China and the U.S. to recognize one another and be friendly, most people in the U.S. assumed China was just an associate of Russia.

As Chairman of the Committee on State Departments Activities and Embassies etc., I went to China soon after Kissinger and Nixon arranged friendly relations. I was there with the right to go wherever I wanted in case we might want to establish a legation there. We were in agreement that there would be five U.S. offices in China—an Embassy in Beijing and four Legation offices spread around the country.

One place I went to was Chungking. No foreigner had been there since the Russians left soon after the war ended. I witnessed great hardships in living conditions. I said I wanted to see a factory, so they showed me a steel factory. I arranged to have several photos taken with the working factory behind me. I brought them back and the U.S. Department of Commerce and people were shocked. China had the most modern steel factory in the world, and sold steel to Finland, which was superior in quality to U.S. steel. The U.S. factories were still open hearth and using iron ore from mines they owned in Brazil. Chinese factories were mixing old steel in with the new. This made it clear that China was making production of commodities its top priority ahead of providing better living conditions to its citizens. China did not have a Communist government tied to Russia. Though they were both Communist, they were not close associates operating under the same economic ideology.

As the Chairman of a sub-committee in the House where appropriations for the State Department and Commerce begin, we were funding expenditures for U.S. employees all over the world. It was very important that members of the committee travelled to see how the employees were performing and to determine the efficiency of their spending. My travels with some members of the committee, and usually a Deputy Secretary for that Department, took us to 80 countries, spending at least three days in each country. The usual procedure was to spend one day examining the facilities and what they were doing, then spending that evening with the U.S. companies doing business in the country, and spending one day examining our relationships with people in that country. I also went to some of the larger countries several times. One country we went to was Lebanon, where we discovered we were not welcome. I was chairing an information meeting. I felt that U.S. soldiers were in great danger personally and were not welcomed by the Lebanese people. I came back to Congress and publicly reported that I thought our troops should leave Lebanon immediately, but the Reagan Administration did not heed my warning. Three weeks later, 230 of our soldiers were killed. The Reagan Administration then removed the whole base from the area. That whole area will probably continue to be a major area of conflict, and with the weapons we have in the world today, and the religious differences and prejudices involved, it is a very dangerous potion brewing.

The 1960s under LBJ were an active period for me. It was a period in which I passed what I considered a backlog of legislation, which I started working on as soon as I came to Congress. One very important law was the Commodity Futures Trading Commission Law. Under it, those needing to acquire commodities, such as corn and wheat, in the future were put into contract with those who would be raising it to sell. Before it passed, elevators covered the risk. The law immediately reduced the risk for both future buyers and sellers of the product. The Commission that was established to administer the law, however, let gamblers in who had no future need for the commodity. They also gave out contracts for non-commodities that should have been placed under the Securities and Exchange Commission. After leaving Congress, I advised Hungary on how to set up a CFTC in their independent nation.

I also succeeded in getting several bills passed in the 1960's that I had discovered were badly needed when I practiced law and when I represented the Packing House Workers. Three of the most important bills I authored in my 36 years in Congress were finally passed in 1967 after eight years of very, very strong and highly financed opposition. They were The Meat Inspection Act, The Poultry Inspection Act, and The Egg Inspection Act. I was the principal sponsor with Congressmen Tom Foley and then Senator Walter Mondale as valuable co-sponsors.

The three acts deal with both economic and health issues and have saved many thousands of people from a serious illness or death. They also protect producers and processors of clean food from unfair competition.

Examples of results include: stopping the mixing of tons of kangaroo meat with some beef and selling it as beef; poultry processors no longer running the feather removal and gut removal so fast that feces was spread on the carcasses (what didn't soak into the meat was washed off); requiring that cattle carcasses be moved on an 18-foot-high rail with the carcasses hanging at least 2 feet off the floor, resulting in no longer having meat wipe the floor and also reducing back injuries. After 1967, 115 plants in Mexico and other countries that had been profiting from selling bad products were closed.

A Des Moines Register reporter Nick Kotz received a Pulitzer Prize for excellent reporting over those years, revealing the facts of the meat processing industry and efforts involved to fix it.

seven

Lessons About Health Care, Medical Research, & Human Survival

Cost of health care is a major problem that has developed in my lifetime. Though we have, through research, made major progress in solving some of our citizens' health problems through vaccinations and correcting ineffective procedures, the costs of health care have increased to the point that they now cover about 18 percent of the total cost of life in the U.S. A major portion of that cost is for people living with disabilities who, through no fault of their own, need major care and do not have the money to pay for it. We should never deny care to anyone who needs it. We need a source of funds other than the health insurance premiums of well, able-bodied people to pay for health care for all.

At present, humans are using oil, minerals and other things accumulated within the earth over the ages. There should and could be a way to divert more income from mining operations and the use of those resources to pay for part of national health care costs associated with the consumption. When valium was produced in the 1950s, some patients in state insane asylums were sent to live at the county farms that had been established during the Great Depression in the county they came from and were given valium in place of professional care at the asylums.

One of the Appropriation Committees I chaired in Congress funded the National Institute of Health research project. When I was on the Committee in 1962, it funded research that totaled $4 billion. The usual research health project lasts something like nine years and needs to last that long because we don't simply need to discover how the find new medicines and ways to benefit the vast majority of people needing medical help but also what harm the remedies for most can do to some. There are generally 3 percent of people who have serious adverse reactions to medicines that are help the other 97 percent of people. As populations increase, we require adequate health research. Some of the medical procedures and responses used in the past were simply wrong. An example of incorrect medical practices was the practice of covering my father's boil with Denver Mud to keep it from coming to a head and draining, resulting in kidney failure. Very soon after I joined the Committee, we started funding almost all of those research projects that the Committee thought showed reasonable promise for success. By the time I left Congress we were appropriating $30 billion per year.

Medical research has saved many lives, but it must be closely monitored. There are members of the Committee that selects the research projects that have a conflict of interest and let that affect their decisions, but research in general is necessary. There must be people appointed to the Committee who know and have dealt in the subject matter. Unfortunately, committee members are often the ones financially involved in the subject being researched. The Committee has to give reports and hearings on current research grants and results. Unfortunately, there are times when the types of

Subcommittee Chairman at the desk.

research projects the Committee approves do more to serve their own financial interests than they do to serve the health needs of U.S. citizens.

One example of this was in a study done on red wine. One day the Chairman of the National Institutes of Health reported to our committee that they had concluded a research project that proved that drinking a modest amount of red wine each day was good for adults. This meant, automatically, that those who did not drink red wine were worse off than those who did.

I asked them how drinking wine compared to drinking the same amount of red grape juice. They had not even included grape juice in the study. My grandmother knew that grape rinds of any color contain a property that has the same positive effect that they were reporting for red wine. She canned grape juice and gave it to us children to help with our indigestion. It wasn't the alcohol in the wine that was helping the people in the study; it was the property in the grape rinds. Promoting a project to determine the effect of red wine that did not include the same study of red grape juice was either a result of a plan to help promote the red wine industry and the result of a conflict of interest. Or perhaps the members of the committee were too dumb to know they were being used by the red wine industry. They changed the official results accordingly, but I still to this day see claims made in reports, including those in magazine reporting, about not only the benefits to be enjoyed from consuming red wine but also the loss of benefits if one doesn't drink wine.

It is an example of the continuing need for members of Congress to not only pass and repeal laws but to be critical in how they are being executed. It is also an example of how necessary the office and funding of the staff of the Inspector General is. I was instrumental in creating that office as a result of the hearings I was involved in in the late 1950s involving Billy Sol Estes and the Department of Agriculture.

I never consumed alcoholic drinks, used tobacco, or used non-prescribed drugs. I never even drank coffee. I am really concerned with the increase in alcohol consumption in this country and the harmful use of non-prescription drugs. But perhaps this increase

Standing in front of the Neal Smith National Wildlife Refuge
with the former Secretary of the Interior, Sally Jewel.

in destructive habits is a part of Nature's way of reducing the
overpopulation of humans.

My century has seen an explosion in human population. The
world is over populated, with six or seven billion people, and
population is increasing fast. Naturally, we want areas with food
shortages to receive the capacity to produce or trade to secure more
food, but that also increases the population excess.

The population explosion is not limited to countries like the
U.S. that has unbelievable new technology; it also applies to Russia,
who increased its population 50 per cent between 1880 and 1910.
With the increased ability to travel worldwide, humans are also
showing a greater increase in migration.

Nature has a powerful ability to balance itself. Whether it is on
the Neal Smith Wildlife Refuge, with plants and small animals, or
with the humans in the world, nature is able to balance itself. I am

fully convinced that the huge difference in activities and population has already resulted in some climate change, and there will be more climate change in the near future. But unlike some people on the climate change side of the debate, I don't think all climate change is or will be bad if we humans change with it. It will obviously affect Iowa agriculture as growing seasons change and move further north. That can be both good and bad. Climate change will have some effect on agriculture all over the world, but I don't think anyone really knows whether it will be a net good or bad for agriculture. Development of new plant species will also be encouraged in the changing weather conditions, especially in farming, and they will have an impact on the entire world's agricultural practices.

A good crop in 1937 and lower prices rallied those supporting acreage allotments and export subsidies, and both were authorized. There is no way to administer allotments that is not unfair to someone. Those who reduced acreage and were not the cause are penalized, but some people advocated for allotments for many years. Believe it or not, I was the principal opponent who succeeded in killing the bill promoted by the Freeman Administration. A bill was up for passage in the House for establishing allotments based on recent history of acreages.

It was three votes short. I was pressured to change my vote, and if I had, several others would have followed. Speaker Sam Rayburn walked back to my seat and asked me if I was going to change. He did not ask me to. Sam Rayburn would never ask me to change my vote. I said no, and he walked back, took the Chair and declared the bill defeated. That was the last we heard of allotments. Export subsidies and penalties are another story.

eight

Lessons From Issues
Specific to Iowa

I was involved with Iowa Public Television by accident from the time of its origin. I was the Attorney for the Polk County School Board in the early 1950s. The County Superintendent of Schools at the time was Ralph Norris. He was a great leader and was involved in the re-organization of the Southeast Polk School District. The Des Moines Independent School District was one of the only school districts in Polk County that I did not represent in some way during the eight years I practiced law before going to Congress.

The Des Moines School District had a policy Ralph Norris disagreed with. They sent any student with an IQ of 70 or less home with no access to education. They couldn't even learn how to read, write, or count. Norris came up with the idea that if the County School Board, which was supported by a 2.5 mil tax, had the equipment to broadcast, it could hire part-time teachers to broadcast lessons that most of those students could listen to at home to at least learn to read and write, add and subtract, etc. He sent me to Washington, D.C. to see if a broadcasting system was available in army surplus. Senator Gillett, from Iowa, who happened to be my cousin, found one and had it sent to Polk County.

We first had a room in a building in Altoona where teachers could broadcast, but Norris soon made arrangements to have it in a room in the building at 18th and Grand, where Des Moines High School students could come and help. One of the students who helped with it while in high school became the leader at Iowa Public Television 30 years later.

I was in Congress and on the Committee dealing with the allocation of spectrum. I made sure public television had channels. It was a constant battle because private companies wanted all of the available channels and very few members of Congress were willing to oppose them. Around the year 1970 I finally won the battle, and channels were finally assured for IPTV. Dan Miller, the leader in Iowa combined several stations in Iowa to Iowa Public Television over the course of a few years, and it is a great success to this day. I also assured WETA that it would receive the channels it needed, and Public Television has become one of the greatest institutions I can proudly say I helped bring into reality to benefit all ages nationwide.

The Des Moines Recreational River and Greenbelt is a National Park in Iowa, existing along the Des Moines River from Fort Dodge to about one mile below Red Rock Dam. I was the author of the bill that established it in 1985. I think it is the only National Park managed by the Army Corps of Engineers instead of the Interior Department. Since the 120,000 acres in the park primarily consists of land and river covering the Saylorville Dam and Red Rock Dam projects and flood protection for the Des Moines city area were already managed by the Corps, I thought the whole of the park should be managed by the Corps as well, including four camping grounds and boat docks on the east side of the Saylorville pool.

1965 groundbreaking at the Saylorville Dam.

The legal boundary for the Greenbelt is considered by the Corps to include parts of nine different counties. It includes a total of 410,000 acres in Boone, Dallas, Jasper, Hamilton, Mahaska, Marion, Polk, Warren, and Webster County. 120,000 of that is owned by the U.S. Corps, and that 120,000 is what future generations will be tasked with managing.

When I became a candidate for Congress in 1958, I made it one of my objectives to not just be in favor of Red Rock and Saylorville Dams and flood control but also to promote recreational opportunities in those areas. At that time, those who could afford it went to the lakes in northern Iowa or Minnesota for vacations. But for others, there was little opportunity available in the central part of the state to enjoy the great outdoors. Having a place to go on a weekend or with the family is important, not just for family enjoyment but for economic development as well.

I was on an airplane sitting next to a person who asked where I was from. When I told him Des Moines, Iowa. He said," I have been there. I had a company in Chicago and needed to relocate. One place I went was Des Moines and met with the Chamber of Commerce. I had about 65 key employees and I needed a place they would want to move to. The Chamber spent their time telling me I should come to Des Moines because Iowa had a right to work law, but that wasn't something those employees would welcome." I asked him where he moved to instead, and he said Cleveland, Ohio. "The reason most said they would be willing to move to Cleveland," he said, "was because there was boating and outdoor recreation available for weekend adventures." Outdoor recreation has economic value.

Rathbun Lake was located in a Congressional District represented by Steve Carter in 1959. He was promoting a dam and service area on the Rathbun River. The bill, which included funding for both Red Rock and Rathbun, was vetoed by President Eisenhower. The leadership in Congress determined that they could pass my bill for Red Rock over the veto but not the one for Rathbun.

Congressman Carter was diagnosed with cancer, and knew he would not complete his term. I told him that although his project was not in the district I represented, I would see to it that it became law. It took a few years, but I was able to keep my word to him. I secured the funding for the Rathbun Lake project, but I considered Steven Carter to be the person most responsible for that worthy project.

In 1959, The Des Moines Chamber opposed Red Rock Dam and that their interest was instead for increasing the number of women living in Des Moines to fill bookkeeper and other administrative job positions for insurance companies and other companies. Thankfully, by the 1970s, the Chamber had undergone a 180-degree change in their focus and instead became a very strong advocate for recreation and the outdoor recreation assets I supported.

The planning and design work for the Red Rock Dam and numerous other dam projects in the U.S. were done during the depression, but Saylorville was not one of them. I secured funding for Red Rock two months after my first year in Congress and set for Saylorville to start in 1965. We needed to develop campgrounds. The Iowa State Department of Natural Resources did not want to construct campgrounds, but they also opposed federal campgrounds because they said it was under their jurisdiction. I had the Corps of Engineers construct four campgrounds at Saylorville on their land. Those are the only campgrounds the Corps operates. Other campgrounds all over the U.S. are operated by the Interior Department. I thought since the Corp owned the land and other operations, they should also run the campgrounds.

In Congress, there are authorizing committees and separate appropriations committees. In general, an authorizing committee for public works may work for years determining whether a project is cost effective and necessary. If a project is approved, it may not be funded by appropriations until years later. Red Rock Dam had been authorized in the depression era but it was not immediately funded. As soon as I took office in 1959, I secured funding and had it constructed over a period of a few years. After it was constructed and in operation, I secured funding and promoted the creation of recreation and camping facilities.

I also started working on the Saylorville project immediately, but it required a substantial amount of research and engineering. The groundbreaking occurred in 1965. Before Saylorville Dam was in operation, Des Moines suffered flooding East and South of West 5th so much that building owners did not even try to keep up their buildings anymore. After Saylorville Dam was constructed, those old buildings were mostly destroyed and a new area was built that included a new Federal Court House. Unlike most cities, Des Moines has a new city constructed within a city. Most other cities in the nation that are the size of Des Moines have a slum area, but Des Moines does not.

The 120,000 acres in Saylorville, Des Moines, Red Rock area, and the recreation areas, including bike trails and boating, now make up a National Destination Park. Unlike most National Parks, a family can come to Des Moines and enjoy a different piece of the Park.

The authorization committee is made up of selected officers from nine cities and several counties. They meet and discuss possible improvement projects. For example, the Principal Insurance Company secured a matching grant authorized by the National Park Service for a river walk they funded for Des Moines. I worked every year I was in Congress in some way on these Des Moines River projects, and seeing them in operation makes me feel all my work was worthwhile. I'm glad I chose to serve in Congress instead of practicing law.

The Skunk River Dam in Ames was being flooded and they needed a sewage disposal system, water supply, and other benefits that a dam project would provide. I secured a $7 million appropriation that would have been all they needed for the project in 1971.

General Schwarzkopf in his headquarters in Saudi Arabia
during the Persian War in 1991.

Interstate 35 was rerouted before it was constructed to accommodate a reservoir. Everything was ready to go, but the legislature went through redistricting in 1972, and Ames and that part of the Skunk River was no longer part of the district I represented in 1963 when the construction was set to begin. According to the rules, since the dam was not in my district, the Governor could object and veto the project. The Governor did so, and the dam was not constructed in 1973 and 1974.

Ten years later, Ames and the surrounding area were again part of the district I represented, but by that time, Ames had constructed a sewer system and water supply and other systems that help to make a dam a good investment. The new estimate would cost $38 million and would not meet the required cost-benefit requirements. Ames has suffered far more damage than the $7 million it would have cost to construct it in 1971.

I was a member of the Izaak Walton League, which held meetings and was active in supporting natural resources and species in particular. Ralph Schlenker and a friend of his were also members and were very active in the League. Ralph was active in supporting technology research I was involved with at Iowa State University. He was also a member of the Board at the Iowa Power and Light Company. I asked Ralph and his friend to look for a place to create a wildlife refuge that would be big enough to include not only bison and elk, but all the sub species that existed as the indigenous land of Iowa—as it was before settlers replaced the natives in the tall green prairie. Iowa and Connecticut have the least amount of reserved public land in the country. Restoring such a refuge would make it the only one in the U.S.

One day Ralph called and said the Board of Iowa Power had just had a meeting and decided not to continue planning for a nuclear plant. They decided to sell the 3,622 acres they had acquired for that purpose. I asked him to find out if they would sell it for the purposes of creating a refuge. The price would have to be fair market price under Federal Law. He inquired and the board agreed to cooperate in that objective.

In 1990, we had an appropriation bill in Conference that had passed both the House and Senate. I succeeded in attaching an amendment to appropriate $6 million, at that very time, for purchasing the land and described in one paragraph what it would be used for. The description skipped years of hearings and reports and both authorized and funded acquisition of the refuge.

The Department of Interior was very much opposed to the idea. They contracted with an appraiser that gave them an appraisal for a ridiculous price of $800 an acre; they said it was of low value because it was so many acres and supported the appraisal by showing where a father sold his daughter a large acreage for less. I asked Iowa Power if they would allow me getting a law passed to condemn the land so that the court would appoint appraisers. They agreed, and it was condemned. The court appointed appraisers gave a more honest appraisal, and it thus became the Iowa National Wildlife Refuge in October 1991. The Federal Government makes an annual payment in lieu of taxes roughly equal to what the taxes would have been, even though there are no school costs.

The Interior Department at first opposed such a restoration project, but after only about three years, they discovered it was very valuable to them. In restoring the land, they discovered some things they should not do in maintaining their 500 refuges in other states. It is also valuable to the state of Iowa. One day I was down there and saw six vans full of visitors on the refuge. Each one was working on a separate research project. The refuge had over 200,000 visitors in 2016. Though it will not be fully restored in my century, or even in the 21st century, the Iowa National Wildlife Refuge is on its way to full restoration. After I left Congress, some former colleagues of mine renamed it The Neal Smith Wildlife Refuge.

I also had secured an appropriation for a facility where Scouts and other youth organizations could stay overnight and study the species living on the Refuge. The plan was to allow them to put up cameras on some areas where the species are active and also where they could go in person into the prairie to observe the wildlife. The year after I left Congress, the appropriation was repealed. If I had been there, I would not have permitted that to happen. It would be so valuable to have such a facility on the Refuge, as there is no other similar place available to the Scouts.

The land secured from the Power Company was 3600 acres, but the Congressional authorization was for all the land drained into Walnut Creek, which totals 11,000 acres. Land has since been acquired from willing sellers and now totals 6200 acres.

The Refuge has a wonderful local volunteer group that supports it and funds young volunteers. The Friends group holds numerous educational events each year. The refuge had 208,540 visitors in 2017 who signed the guest book and 7,660 school children who spent a day at the refuge. 147 Monarch Butterflies were tagged, and 331 acres were added. It has already been a great success, but it will continue to add species and work toward returning it to the way it used to be.

Gray's Lake and Brown's Woods are two great assets for the Des Moines area that were not named when they came up for sale in an Estate. They were not originally planned as public parks. The city of Des Moines had planned to fill in an old gravel pit that the original estate owned, and the 500 acres of woods was for sale. The eastern half of what is now Gray's Lake was owned by the City and the old federal building and some other junk had been dumped in it. What is now Brown's Woods was as 500-acre timber plot that has never been cut. It is a real gem that somehow managed to survive while the cities around it were being developed.

I thought they both could be great public parks. They had caught my attention when I was looking for a place to construct a dam on the Raccoon River. I found that the only place there might be a dam constructed that would meet the cost-benefit ratio requirements was up by Jefferson. That would not protect the Des Moines area, so I felt a park area was needed in the Raccoon River area specifically.

I called the administrator of the estate involved. I determined that the Estate really did not need the huge sums those assets could bring if sold to developers. I suggested that they sell it cheap to turn into parks that would be named for Gray and Brown. Brown agreed and said they could sell for as little as one million dollars—$500,000 for each.

I searched for a program with Federal Funds. There was an old, expired program that had $500,000 left in funds when it was ready to expire. It was a matching grant program. I had the program declared unexpired so that we could use it for these opportunities. That meant we needed local support for a $250,000 match for each asset.

I called the Downtown Business Group, and they said they would support the gravel pit acquisition. I called the Polk County Conservation Group and they immediately agreed and conducted fundraising activities for the matching grant for Brown's Woods with an obligation to keep it as an original timber forest and used only as an natural park with the name Brown's Woods.

Months later, I received a call from the federal agency saying they had not received the money for the Gray's property, and the funding would not be available after the fiscal year ended—only three weeks from then. I found out the Des Moines Business Group wanted to let investors buy it instead.

I preferred to carry out the agreement with Brown to make it a Gray's Lake Park. I knew that the Des Moines Women's Club, which Bea belonged to, had on several occasions supported park projects. I called them, and they immediately agreed to raise the matching grant. In two weeks' time, the Des Moines Women's Club raised the money needed for the matching funds to make it Gray's Lake Park.

Several years later, the city council held a meeting to convert it into a commercial location for gambling boat operation. That would have wielded our agreement we made with the Brown Estate.

30 members of the Des Moines Women's Club appeared with me at the council meeting and they convinced the council to not violate the agreement with the Brown Estate.

The Des Moines Women's Club deserves credit for making Gray's Lake Park and keeping it the great recreation area it is today.

Drake University is a great institution. Nine members of my immediate family have received part or most of their education from there, including Bea and my law degrees, which we earned in 1950. I have always been so appreciative of the U.S. having a Constitution that, for longer than in any other country, has protected the rights of individuals and prohibited someone who is elected President from trampling on the rights of others or of continuing in office past the term for which they were elected. I have also strongly believed everyone should have access to the legal representation they need to be treated properly. I am pleased to have had an opportunity to help Drake University contribute to that cause.

The Drake Law School Court Room is used at least a few times each year for legal proceedings and is available to both students and the public. The funding for its construction included requirements such as a place to sit and write for a crowd and an opportunity for the public to experience and come to appreciate our legal system. The Drake Law School Court Room fully met my expectations.

Drake needed $8 million for a law library and $10 million to allow pharmacy students to have individual stations and classrooms. I was interested in both, and decided to participate in a fundraising campaign. For the Bicentennial of the Constitution, I thought it important to have at least four law schools hold public lectures each year on Constitutional matters of current interest. I was pleased to be able to make Drake Law one of those four national institutions. It is important that we use the facilities of the Law School to provide an opportunity for students to be involved in some very educational ways while also providing legal services for those who need financial help, and I am pleased to have been involved in providing that.

Drake University has been very helpful to Bea, me, and our family, and I am pleased to have been a contributor in time, effort, and finances to that great institution.

The University of Iowa is a great university that I am pleased to have been able to help several times. Once, I succeeded in securing the National Advanced Driving Simulator. Michigan wanted it badly, and some auto companies wanted it in Michigan, but I was able to require it to be located at the University of Iowa.

It became an $80 million program. I did not realize it would cost that much, but I drove the simulator and was amazed at what it can do to make someone react as though they were driving 70 miles an hour. The University of Iowa helped me to understand some things I needed to know when I chaired the Committee funding the National Institutes of Health, and I am glad I was able to add their representation to the National Committee on Grants.

Iowa State University is likewise a tremendous asset to the State of Iowa, and I am glad to have had an opportunity to help them obtain a total of about $200 million in grants over a period of about 25 years. There are so many programs and opportunities that are only available if there is an effort to be a beneficiary, and there are so many ways for an institution to partner with private businesses for mutual benefit. I was in a position to help with appropriations and was also Chairman of the Small Business Committee. As such, is always looking for ways to help start businesses in the state.

In the mid 1970s, Ames badly needed a new Vet School. Bob Parks was President of the University at the time. I teamed up with Congressman Shriver, a Republican member from Kansas, and secured a $25 million matching grant for each State Vet School. A big lobby group noticed our efforts and secured what they thought was the political help it needed to be a lobbyist for Iowa State. It was proposed to Bob Parks at a Board of Regents Meeting. Bob called me, and I told him I was not working for a lobbyist and that he should hire someone to be in his office who I could know for certain would speak for him. He hired Mike Crow. Mike was a genius at thinking of ways Iowa State could be a greater asset for jobs and economic gain to help new startup businesses and increase opportunities for beginning businesses. I secured funding when needed to create those opportunities, but the funding did not always come from existing national programs.

We started a program to transfer new technology to either new or established businesses. It needed some financial help from the state government. They were not interested, even though it would return far more to the state than the initial cost. Technology transfer was such a good program that the state government finally promised to participate if I could get it funded for the first five years. I did just that at an annual total cost of about $6 million per year. It was obviously returning far more than that, but it wasn't a State Program and the State Appropriations bills did not fund it as promised. I had it funded an extra four years, and I went to the Legislature and personally presented proof that it was profitable for the Iowa government to partner with new and old businesses, but the state legislature, governor, and a new board of regents did not approve it to continue.

Bob Parks then retired and Gordon Eaten became the new President of Iowa State. The new state board of regents prohibited Eaton from budgeting the program. Eaton resigned, and they opened the search for a new Iowa State President. No truly qualified person applied; all qualified applicants refused to apply when they found out why Eaten had resigned. The new board of regents recruited Martin Jischke.

Mike Crow, who worked for Bob Parks, went to Columbia University and had great success there. He is now the President of Arizona State. The new Research Park was Mike Crow's idea, and I secured funding for it. It has been expanded to includes a substantial number of companies that find the location and access to Iowa State resources very profitable. Iowa State received an award for securing fifteen significant patents in one year, which was more than any other similar institution. Eleven of those patents came from the Transfer Program. In the years when Bob Parks, Eaton, and Mike Crow were at Iowa State, along with that a particular Board of Regents, we did far more to increase educational and economic opportunities and causes in Iowa than that which was accomplished in any other prior century.

Iowa State University is a great Iowa asset and holding the positions I held in the House gave me opportunities to help that I would not have held if I were in the Senate. I had at least two opportunities to run for the Senate and I likely would have been elected, but I would have lost the positions I had in the House due to losing my seniority. It was worth it to me to stay in the House for 36 years. Other programs we started or began participating in during my time in Congress included a National Soil Tilth Lab, Micro-electronics Research Center, Human Nutrition Center, Center for Ag and Rural Development, Fossil Energy Lab, Center for Non-destructive Evaluation, Aviation Systems Reliability, Food and Agriculture Policy Institute, Animal Science and Food Consortium with Arkansas and Kansas State, Midwest Center for Aquaculture, and Soybean Bi-processing.

I was the chairman of the Small Business Committee in the House for many years. It came to our attention that while some small businesses succeeded and provided both jobs and income to the economy, and a big increase in the income paid in taxes to governments, about one half of all new small businesses failed. We conducted a three-year study to determine why so many businesses failed. In some cases, there was no need for them to exist at all, but in many cases it was because they needed some management help they could not afford. At the same time, we had small business government loans involved in some cases. Colleges and universities were teaching courses in which students need actual experience, which could have been provided by those small businesses as a part of the students' education while giving the business the help it needed as well.

We devised what is called a Small Business Development Program and passed the law. It was funded in 1980. Under the SBDC program, small businesses could receive one-on-one counseling and low cost training from experienced business professionals from the private sector. They could also get college resources, including students in business classes, development of business plans, manufacturing assistance, financial packaging assistance, contracting both national and international trade assistance, technology transfer advice, and market research assistance.

The program has been a great success. It is administered by a lead service center in each state and by other local service centers. In Iowa, the lead center is headquartered at Iowa State University, and we set up 25 local service centers around the state. By the time of the National Silver Anniversary in 2005 in Baltimore, where I was honored, there were 1100 local centers in the U.S., D.C, Puerto Rico, the Virgin Islands, Guam, and the American Samoa. Funding for the program came from a federal grant with a partial match by states that participated in the program. A study showed that for each dollar of tax money spent, federal and state governments received $4 more than they would have received had the small businesses not being established and successful.

In 2005, 750,000 businesses received services of some kind from the program, and they created 160,000 jobs nationwide. In the first 25 years, the program had served over 11 million clients for new business start-ups, struggling firms, or business expansions. There is a committee appointed by small business organizations that is actively engaged in making sure the program is supporting small businesses. At the Silver Anniversary, they announced an annual award that goes to one successful business in each state. It is called The Neal Smith Business Award.

nine

Lessons From Late
20th Century Issues

By 1973, the post war boom was beginning to come to an end. World Trade had grown at 6 percent per year from 1948 until 1960 and by 9 percent from 1960 to 1973. New technology, increased understanding of plant biology, and vast increases in the ability to produce agricultural products for both food and industrial use had increased more than in any previous period in history. With a huge increase in International Commerce, new technology and the increase in ability to produce per human per hour and year had resulted both in profits for investors and reduced leverage for increases in wages for workers. I had worked for less than $2 per day in 1938 on jobs that by 1972 paid far more per hour. Cost of living also skyrocketed, however, and, unlike prior to the depression, non-communist economics in countries around the world were a mixture of both private enterprise and government investment and regulation. We were now entering a period where there would be milder recessions than we had in the 1930s and shorter periods of recovery. Government would be heavily involved in all of it.

People in various countries would naturally want to migrate to whatever country had a better standard of living, and there were numerous problems in government few countries had ever faced before. I was a Member of Congress during this time. While free enterprise economics had own problems, these vast changes led to the collapse of the Communist system, which had lagged far behind. Hungary, which was a part of the Soviet Union, defied the leaders in Moscow, and others in countries in the Union followed. Citizens of Romania murdered the leader and simply left the Soviet Union. Even the country of Estonia, in which the Soviets had built the most efficient seaport in the world, left the union. The other opening to the Western World is the Ukraine port in Crimea, and Ukraine too left the Soviet Union.

The post war boom was about to end, and Nixon was President. He was destined to be a failure in some ways both affecting his tenure and the economy. But he had Kissinger in the Foreign Affairs and the State Department. Kissinger was a great leader in the field of diplomacy and Nixon enacted Kissinger's policies. As we in the U.S. moved toward bad economic times, with interest rates under Carter as high as 15 percent, Russia and China were also having economic problems and were not in a position to continue expensive military costs involved in their efforts to take over other countries. We were obligated to defend those countries and were about to follow the same pattern as the boom that followed WWI and then the major economic problems that came after. Our free enterprise system does not give us the ability to have permanent economic prosperity that works like a clock, but we have a Constitution that prevents temporary leaders from giving themselves permanent authority over the country. The temporary elected government under our

Constitution must continue to preserve the personal rights of the minority and also face a retention vote. We have had rights and protections against dictatorships in our Constitution for longer than any country in the world. It is the ultimate in individual liberty and justice. We should celebrate it every day of the year, not just on the 4th of July. By comparison, the Russian Communist System has failed in both human rights and economically.

Mikhail Gorbachev became the leader in the Soviet Union in 1985. His rise to power was a surprise to our Foreign Affairs Intelligence. They had assumed leadership would continue with one of the old crowd. Gorbachev had been what we would call the Secretary of Agriculture in our government. One time, when I was on an inspection trip with the Committee I chaired, Gorbachev requested a meeting with me and a Senator from North Dakota, who, like me, was a long time farmer and was interested in farm legislation.

I assumed it would be a short meeting, but I was also curious about how they managed the Reindeer herd they used as a national meat source. I asked him if they fed them hay some years in order to produce a larger herd. They had not thought of that. He became very interested in my opinion about cow and animal herds and how it was possible for farmers in the U.S. to have electricity. The meeting lasted three hours. When he became the leader of the Soviet Union, our intelligence people interviewed me about him. They did not even know if he spoke English. I knew he could speak English because I had tricked him into correcting his interpreter when I asked a question during our meeting.

Gorbachev made a big change in the Russian leadership. He tried to reform the system. He did not want to destroy it but rather make it work better. He wanted more individualism, and there was resistance among the Union, according to our intelligence people.

He even wanted to replace the Union's big party committee with an elected committee. Countries I was visiting in that period, such as Hungary, Romania, and Czechoslovakia, sensed an opportunity to exit the Union under Gorbachev's leadership, and they did so in 1991. The Union also suffered from crime and corruption, but instead of changing their system, they chose a new leader: Boris Yeltsin. Since I chaired the committee that funded most of our diplomatic functions, I went on several inspection tours and became very prominent in questions concerning the Embassy and their agricultural capacity.

The 200th birthday of the adoption of the U.S. Constitution and Bill of Rights occurred in 1986. A Commission was established to celebrate the event over a period of about five years. Chief Supreme Court Justice Warren Burger retired and became the Chairman of the Commission. I was the Chairman of the Appropriations Sub-Committee that appropriated $12 million for the funding of the commission, and I worked closely with Chief Burger. I have numerous communications personally signed by him.

In a lasting contribution during this Commission, we established four grants, of $800,000 each, at four law schools to fund annual seminars about current Constitution problems or matters of national interest. One of the Constitution Law Centers is at Drake University in Des Moines, Iowa.

During the George H. W. Bush Administration, Newt Gingrich became active and was moving toward being the new leader. That was when the divisive movements in the Republican Party began. Instead of taking advantage of the situation, a bare majority in the Democratic Party, which were from safe districts, started trying to force the minority to fall in line. As a result, the Democrats lost their majority for the first time in 40 years. The Supreme Court united decision also passed about the same time.

Justice O'Connor and Justice Powell.

Justice Scalia.

Justice Warren.

The drive by Gingrich to become the Republican leader continued into 1992, Ross Perot ran for President during the Republican vote Bush needed for re-election. Bill Clinton was elected with 43 percent of the total vote. I had known the Clintons since 1980, and when I was not re-elected in 1994, I could have had a very good Ambassadorship or some other appointment. However, I wanted to be one of the few to leave completely. I instead did consulting for Lithuania when they joined the European Union and needed to be able to sell healthy dairy products. I also consulted for

Hungary and spent a week there setting up a Commodity Futures Trading Commission. I also spent about two weeks consulting at the Marshall Center in Germany.

The U.S. Supreme Court and all the federal courts were also funded by appropriation bills developed and passed by the subcommittee I chaired while in Congress. The U.S. Supreme Court is the overall administrator of U.S. Courts. It does not merely deal with cases referred to it for decisions. It also has important, time-consuming administrative obligations.

At least three or four Members of the Court testified each year to the sub-committee I chaired. All appropriations for all the U.S. Courts were funded by that sub-committee. I was in a very unique spot with my personal relationships with the U.S. Supreme Court members, not in any way involving their court decisions but very much in dealing with the funding needed for the Courts. The U.S. Courts have two national meetings in a big room in the Supreme Court each year for reports and general planning that are Chaired by the Chief Justice. Seventy-five representatives of various levels of courts and all nine districts sit around an oval table. I was invited to sit about ten feet behind the Chief Justice. That was so that I would be aware of any Administrative programs that came up. It was a unique opportunity to see how the Courts operate. One day, Supreme Court Chief Justice Renquist announced that in the next year the Supreme Court would decide 85 appeals instead of the usual 112 in the past. The Courts have recently reduced that number further. Changes in numerous laws and technologies have greatly increased the load and importance of cases in the U.S. Court system.

The U.S. Supreme Court has made decisions on very few cases that need to be corrected by a Constitutional Amendment or some other drastic measure, but there are a few of note. One bad decision happened at the beginning of WWII that held that U.S. citizens could be moved to a special campground in Utah if they were of Japanese descent. The anti-Japanese feeling was very strong after Pearl Harbor in February 1942. FDR issued an Executive Order that forced 110,000 American Citizens of Japanese descent to move to the camp in Utah.

Fifty years later, Congress passed a law authorizing each one of the citizens who was forced into the camp to receive $20,000 in restitution, but that was just an authorization measure. The majority in Congress would not vote for a separate appropriation to pay it. That failure lasted for more than three years. I decided I would take the leadership on it. The payout would total $2 billion. An appropriation bill from the committee I chaired had passed in both the House and the Senate. Senator Hollings of North Carolina was the chairman of the committee handling the bill in the Senate. I told him I thought we should pay it, and he agreed. We added $2 billion to the bill that had passed both Houses and secured the votes to pass it in Congress.

Another rare Supreme Court Decision that I strongly criticized was the decision in 2000 that declared George W. Bush the winner when the votes were not all counted in an election contest. I think it was wrong to name him the winner at that time.

One decision the Court made that I think should be corrected was the Citizens United Decision on January 21, 2010. It held that corporations, unions, and some other entities can spend unlimited amounts of money for advertising and other activities influencing elections because, they said, spending that money is a form of Constitutionally protected free speech. Since this political spending in campaigns could not be equally curtailed, cost of elections has skyrocketed to millions of dollars each race, and it is the amount of advertising that often determines the outcomes of elections. It will take a Constitutional Amendment to correct that decision.

ten

The Biggest Changes
in My Century

No one could have ever dreamed we would have the huge change in communications technology that occurred between 1920 and today. Telephones in the country in 1920 were eight parties on one line connected by a person in a community telephone office. Each party had an assignment of a number of rings necessary to call them. City telephone service was also connected only by wire lines. Calling someone any distance away was a difficult, if not impossible, task. Today, on the other hand, we are able to call someone in a second, and the call may go to a satellite and down to another party in another country. I don't understand how many of those forms of communication work, but it is like magic. There has been more progress made in communications in the last century than in all previous centuries.

Another one of the biggest changes in my century was the increase in the size of farms and the amount of production per person. As a teenager just out of high school, I rented 40 acres and used my parent's horses and machinery. They were farming 108 acres, and our two plots together were more than most families farmed. One of the limitations we ran into was in harvesting corn. When it was all done by hand—one ear at a time—in the 1920s, we were limited on how much we could farm. I could harvest as much as 150 bushels per day. I even entered a contest when I was 18, but the average was more like 75 or 80 bushels per day.

In the 1920s almost everyone farmed with horses, though a few had a tractor that hardly did more work per day than four horses. Now, after 100 years of progress in farm technology, we have Harvesters that harvest as many acres in one day as we raised in the 1920s on one farm.

eleven

The Key Lessons to Learn From My Century

We will soon be in the last year of my century. It is time to recall the changes that have occurred and to consider whether they were for good or ill for the state and country as a whole. The answer is that they were far greater in number and consequence than could have been expected and they were in almost every case both good and bad in some respect. A huge percentage of these changes in this century were never before even dreamed of.

New technologies discovered and developed and the ability to recover from the earth huge amounts of energy in various forms created in previous thousands of years. The development of natural resource usage systems has been greater than in any other century of Earth history.

Development has occurred in my century in other ways as well, for good and ill in my opinion: In 1920, farms in Iowa were mostly 80 or 120 acres in size. My great grandfather paid $1.25 per acre for land when he moved to Iowa in 1850. Today, land sells for

2014, at age 94 standing in front of the gate at
my childhood home.

thousands of dollars per acre, but a dollar with inflation make the comparison irrelevant.

In 1920, farmers needed only horses and mules for farming work. An average farm was on a mud road; it raised a few hogs and butchered and cured meat one per family member and sold the rest; it had four or five milk cows and farmers sold the cream the family did not need; it had a chicken flock consisting of 100 hens for eggs and a chicken to eat on each Sunday; and farmers raised no more corn than a farmer could shuck one ear at a time by hand. In 2016, on the other hand, the average farm in the U.S. averaged around 442 acres.

I started in the 1st grade when I was four years old; today children are in some kind of pre-school for one or two years followed by Kindergarten before they enter first grade. I went to school in a "hack" pulled by horses on a dirt road. We expected that we would catch several diseases, like mumps and measles, that children are vaccinated for today. In each community in the county and each neighborhood in the cities, people were either immigrants or the children of immigrants, and all were very much prejudiced in favor of their own ethnic group and religion. Growing up, I never expected to travel to 80 or more counties and serve in the war as I did. I never expected to go anywhere a train was not able to travel.

Farm children like me had at least two dogs. They met us when we got off the hack from school and watched the babies like they thought someone might harm them. On farms and in rural towns, we also had pets like raccoons and crows. We understood that there are sub-species that we all depend on. We understood, almost inherently, that there was an ecosystem that included hundreds of other species. Today, I have witnessed city children, from Des Moines especially, who first discover there are other species when they visit the Neal Smith Wildlife Refuge.

The atomic bomb had never been imagined by most scientists with doctoral degrees until it was dropped on Japan in WWII. Since the day it was used, it is possible that someone somewhere in the world will use that source of energy or some other explosive or chemical component to kill a lot of people. Though it had such a major influence in the outcome of the war, I can't label the bomb a positive change that occurred in my century.

As late as college, I had never heard of the kinds of communications we now have; and I never would have imagined that I would know before the Soviets did that we could hear what they were saying in a low-area building from a satellite. The increase in communications is both good and bad—life-saving and life-threatening.

Our entertainment in Packwood growing up was the local basketball team or the orchestra in the city bandstand or school.

Today we see on TV what was only in my childhood available in New York or Hollywood.

I simply do not understand how to receive a lot of the social media that is available on my iPhone, let alone how it is possible that the two first trillionaires in the U.S. were people raised in normal families like mine who invented and patented how to send a message to a satellite and back to Earth in two seconds. Time has become more valuable late in my century than it seemed earlier in my century, but that has as much to do with perception as it does with progression.

It has been a century since March 23, 1920. And it has been a century like no other century my generation could ever had imagined. Nothing can ever be labelled entirely good or entirely bad, even in hindsight. But my hope is that, if nothing else, generations of the future will use the knowledge of the history of my century to make choices for the greater good of people alive in theirs.

INDEX

Throughout this index, the abbreviation N.E.S. will be used to indicate references to Neal Edward Smith. Page numbers appearing in italic type refer to pages that contain photographs.

assistance, 5–6, 10–11
research programs for, 12
Russian interest in Iowan
methods, 41–42, 56, 89
technological improvements
and, 6–7, 87, 95–96
Federal income tax, 3
Federal Securities Act (1933), 10
First Amendment, 94
flood protections, 71–76
4-H clubs, 12–13
France
Middle Eastern conflicts,
involvement in, 36
Southeast Asian protectorates,
leaving, 44, 51
free enterprise system
criticism of, 11, 16, 41
Great Depression and, 1, 9, 11,
16, 17
success of, 39, 88–89
unemployment issues and, 17,
35
WWII and, 18
free speech, 94

Garst, Roswell, 41–42
gas tax, 19
gender
discrimination based on, 27,
38–39
voting rights and, 38, 43
General Agreement on Tariffs and
Trade (GATT), 32
Germany
economic power of, 35

Hitler as Chancellor of, 17
NATO membership, 31
N.E.S. consulting in, 93
oppression of opposition in, 17
post-WWI, 2
post-WWII, 25, 29, 30
WWII and, 17–18
GI Bill (1944), 27
Gillette, Guy, 71
Gingrich, Newt, 90, 92
globalization, 87
gold, prices of, 12
Gorbachev, Mikhail, 56, 89–90
Gray's Lake, Des Moines, 79–80
Great Depression
corn prices and, 1
dust bowl period, 13, 16
free enterprise system and, 1, 9,
11, 16, 17
income tax and, 3
poverty assistance and social
programs during, 4–6, 8–12,
15, 38
presidential election of 1936
and, 13–15
Greece, war in, 32
Grinnell College, 23–24
Gulf of Tonkin Resolution
(1964), 52

Hawley-Smoot Tariff Law (1930),
3
health care
cost of, 64
medical research and, 2, 65–67
for veterans, 56

biggest changes during, 95–96
discrimination and
communism, 38–43
employment and economic
issues, 87–89
health care and medical
research, 64–69
Iowa during, 87–94
lessons from, 97–100
migration, 88
post-WWII lessons, 27–37
Soviet Union, end of, 88–90
Supreme Court decisions,
91–92, 93–94
Vietnam War, 44–52

Ukraine, leaving Soviet Union, 88
unemployment, 5–7, 8, 16, 17,
35
United Kingdom
Indian relations, 36
Israel, establishment of, 37
Middle Eastern conflicts,
involvement in, 36
protectorates, leaving, 44
United Nations
Cold War and, 30, 34
on human rights, 26, 32
Israel, recognition of, 37
NATO, establishment of, 25–26
Universal Declaration of Human
Rights (1948), 26, 32
University of Iowa, 82
University of Missouri, 25, 28
U.S. Army Corps of Engineers
(USACE), 71, 74

Venezuela, restrictions on
elections, 58–59
veterans
GI Bill (1944), 27
health care access, 56
poverty reduction during Great
Depression, 5
veterinarian schools, 82
Vietnam War, 44–52
Agent Orange used during, 49
battle tactics during, 49–50, *50*
chronology of events, 51–52
ending, 50–52
Gulf of Tonkin Resolution
(1964), 52
precursors to, 44–46
protection from communism,
43–44, 48–52
U.S. military deaths resulting
from, 46
voting and voting rights, 38, 43

Wallace, Henry, 11–12
Walnut Creek, 78
Warren, Earl, *92*
Whitten, Ed, 20
Willkie, Wendell, 16
wine, research on, 66–67
women. *See* gender
Works Program Administration
(WPS), 10, 16
World War I
cost of, 3
punishment of Germany for, 2
veterans, bonuses for, 5

Made in the USA
Coppell, TX
09 September 2020